Land of the Goat

LAND *of the* GOAT

Witchcraft in the Pyrenees

Júlia Carreras Tort

Original images by
MARIANNA ATŁAS

Three Hands Press
2024

Land of the Goat

First Three Hands Press edition, August 2024.

Book design by Joseph Uccello and Daniel A. Schulke.
Typeset by J. Uccello.

ISBN-13: 978-1-945-147-487 (softcover)

Printed in the United States of America.

www.threehandspress.com

Contents

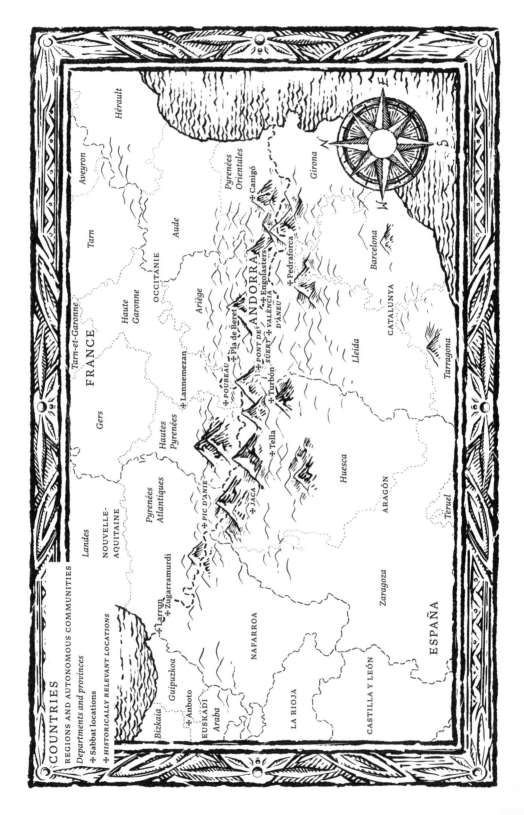

Introduction

The goal of this book is to offer the reader a detailed picture of the primordial aspects of the witch, known as the *bruxa*. This book shall examine how this folkloric, supernatural, and other-than-human witch was perceived prior to the social crises of the late Middle Ages and Early Modern Era, and observe its evolution from the witch craze through to the present times while placing it into the particular context of the Pyrenees.

The book's four main chapters begin with The Witch, uncovering the origins and development of the *strix* or the *hag* and its Pyrenean counterpart, the *bruxa* or *bruja*. Next is The Devil, an introduction to the one who grants the primordial witch its power, an oppugnant but fundamental figure still evident in Pyrenean folklore, and one that deeply influenced moral and religious law. The Land follows, uncovering its role in the supernatural existence and nature-regulating abilities of the *bruxa,* as well as providing the animate setting for the development of the practice of witchcraft. Finally, we join the *ajunt de bruxes* or The Witches' Sabbat to discover the key, the ultimate nexus between the human and the other-than-human worlds, the cyclical apotheosis accessed through the Land.

These four concepts should be understood as interdependent and traditionally related in Pyrenean folklore. The complex layers of overlapping definitions, interpretations, and even limitations of the Witch, the Devil, the Land, and the Sabbat form a single great enigma, moving forward as one. Together they culminate in a conceptual glyph that may be unfolded by the dedicated reader.

GEOGRAPHY, LANGUAGE AND OTHER CHALLENGES

BEFORE continuing, there are some specifics about geography, the treatment of local languages and selections of terms that should be clarified.

I chose to limit the area of the *bruxa* to the Pyrenees because of its idiosyncratic crossroads-like position, harsh climate, and turbulent history. To those unfamiliar with the area, the Pyrenees is a mountain range that separates the Iberian peninsula (where Spain and Portugal are located) from the rest of Europe. It is divided in several regions belonging to different territories: the Catalan, the Aragonese, the Basque and Navarrese Pyrenees, all belonging to the country of Spain, Andorra—an independent country of its own, and the French Pyrenees, divided into different regions as well: Pyrénées-Orientales, Aude, Ariège, Haute-Garonne, Hautes-Pyrénées, and Pyrénées-Atlantiques. Each region, though sharing common cultural features, has idiosyncrasies of its own.

Accordingly, Pyrenean regions are conformed by Aranese, Aragonese, Basque, Catalan, French, and Occitan languages and dialects, something that forced me to choose a nomenclature for the terms I was going to deal with for the sake of coherence and discursiveness. I have chosen the word *bruxa*, in old Catalan form, to represent the primordial Pyrenean witch (also because of its similarity to the more popular Spanish word, *bruja*). Not only because Catalan is my mother tongue, but this Catalan word is now believed to have originated in Pyrenean lands, and it was also the first to appear in written form. Something similar happens with the word *ajunt*, meaning the night gathering or witches' sabbat. The Catalan/Occitan word was chosen over other languages for semantic and etymological reasons, i.e., not being contaminated by anti-Semitic nor anti-heretic propaganda, and for being native to the area and being used systematically by informants—see the explanation on the Basque *akelarre* in the fifth chapter for a more detailed account.

Choosing to translate the word *bruxa* as 'primordial witch' is an attempt to best describe a spirit or entity characterised by its supernatural—other-than-human—nature, forever bound to animistic spirituality. The *bruxa* was once the embodiment of a discarnate taboo, a deviant—yet absolutely necessary—figure inherently linked to the Land, to Death, and the Otherworld. Using the adjective 'primordial' is not meant as derogatory in any way, since the *bruxa* represents an unpolluted, visceral aspect of the Pyrenean quotidian reality.

Another linguistic concern is the deliberate de-gendering of the Devil, for which I will use the pronoun "it" from now on in this book. By granting the pronoun "it" to the Devil, I intend to emphasize the non-humanity of the entity, as it shall be thoroughly examined in its corresponding chapter.

Multiple versions of the same folk tales or legends concerning the supernatural or the *bruxa* also presented challenges. This is especially true of Basque, Catalan, and Navarrese folktales, where stories are often repeated from town to town. Rather than offer an exhaustive catalogue of similar tales, one version of a story was chosen over other versions from different locations, sometimes the oldest or the most popular. Of course, this does not mean that any other versions or areas are less important than the ones quoted, but a choice had to be made in order to facilitate the flow of discourse.

Obsolete sources that claimed to analyze the witchcraft phenomenon in French, Spanish, Basque, Occitan, Aranese, and Catalan have been another sizable challenge. Typically, the primordial witch was too quickly equated with the sorcerer, the magical practitioner, the folk healer, or the poisoner. This lack of analysis on the primordial witch could possibly be attributed to the absence of a global Pyrenean approach in the currently available folklore studies, with notable exceptions. But for a few historians and anthropologists (e.g., Carlo Ginzburg, Claude Lecouteux, Alejandro Campagne, Pau Castell), the implications of the primordial witch in Pyrenean history and anthropology have been vastly overlooked.

The first civil law against witchcraft passed in 1424 has been practically ignored until very recently, and I felt it was time to give this event and its perennial effects the importance they deserve.

Writing a book in English for a non-Pyrenean audience also required special care in faithfully recounting and analyzing these histories. Informants, witnesses, and even those accused during trials expressed themselves in a particularly encoded way of dealing with reality in relation to the *bruxa,* the Devil, the Land, and the *ajunt.* This is why, in some cases, the original Aranese, Basque, Catalan, French, Occitan, or Spanish terms or text segments have been kept in full quotation. The original text is there as a resource that a reader may investigate further, to explore the enigmatic tone of a speaker faced with a reality that he or she is experiencing, but clearly needs protection from.

Perhaps the greatest concern of all was more of a limitation. This book treats phenomena and events which took place in the distant-to-recent past, but which have mainly been documented in the current era. Tackling a phenomenon so crucial in a pre-rationalistic past with a post-rationalistic mindset has, honestly, been quite demanding. A deep process of unlearning and a state of constant doubt, of questioning of everything I encountered, were essential. The more I advanced, though, the more it all seemed to fit. If the theories and lucubrations contained in this book can send the reader on a journey to another time and place, back to the mythical and magical realms of the mind, the intention of this book will be fulfilled.

—Júlia Carreras Tort

Acknowledgements

FIRST OF ALL, TO HECTOR FOR BEING MY
COMPANION IN THE *VIARANY* 'THE CROOKED
PATH'. THIS BOOK IS ALSO HIS.

TO MY GRANDPARENTS AND ANCESTORS, FOR
SHOWING ME THE REALITY-SHAPING ABILITIES
OF TALES, FOR LOVING THEIR WOODLAND
DWELLINGS AND RELATING TO THE LANDS IN
WAYS THAT SHOULD NEVER BE FORGOTTEN.

TO MY FRIENDS, FOR THEIR HELP, AND FOR
BEING A SOURCE OF ENDLESS INSPIRATION
AND COMFORT.

AND TO THE *BRUXA* AND THE PYRENEES,
WHICH GUIDED MY HAND IN TIMES OF
HESITATION AND SHOWED ME THAT HUMANITY
IS LIMITED, WHILE NATURE IS NOT.

CHAPTER I

The History
of the
Primordial Witch

'They go forth by night with the BRUXES*'*

IZENA DON GUZTIE EMEN DA
'ALL THINGS THAT HAVE A NAME DO EXIST'

Ccording to this Basque saying, a thing exists by virtue of having been given a name. The Pyrenean *bruxa*, the primordial witch, was made real through the magic of words, not as a human figure but as an entity of the Underworld that embodied opposition, and posed a threat to daily life. But whose powerful words transformed the nature of this threatening primordial witch from spirit to human? And how did that transformation lead to the first secular law against witchcraft passed in Europe? Let's begin with the primordial aspects of the witch, the original *bruxa*: what was its form and purpose?

Bruxes (plural of "*bruxa*") were considered representatives of the supernatural world. Mountain communities, for their own good, felt compelled to interact with *bruxes* in order to prevent a wild array of misfortunes and maladies. Countless cautionary folktales and apotropaic customs described the power of *bruxes*; how their nocturnal acts could cause nightmares, for example, and how other supernatural entities attended their revelries — including certain human beings capable of detaching their spirits from their bodies, and *flying*. The rumour of these specially empowered humans attending the witches' revelries was the wedge that opened the door to the next phase of the *bruxa*. By the end of the Middle Ages, the theological elites progressively began the *bruxa's* definitive transformation from a supernatural to a human being through a systematic prosecution of superstition, establishing a connection between the *bruxa*, heresy, and folk magic. This conceptual shift contributed to what we now know as the witch craze, a profound crisis during which the *bruxa* became a scapegoat for the social change that preceded the imposition of rationalism. After the witch craze and during the Enlightenment, the *bruxa* would come to represent the embodied victim of a dominating patriarchy. Still, the history of the *bruxa* is much deeper, one that should be taken as part of an ancient mystery that continues to exert its influence beyond particular time frames.

This chapter shall offer a portrait of the primordial aspects of the witch, the *bruxa*, using the Pyrenees region to represent the rural life of mountain communities. By attuning the reader to the pulse of the Land at the time of the *bruxa's* origin, my aim is to approach with a vehement, if cautious, curiosity, revealing the *bruxa* as a nearly lost and yet vital, endemic knowledge. In order to understand the reality and complexity of the Pyrenean *bruxa*, it is imperative to at least contemplate a world in which they were thought to roam. Pyrenean communities share a complex and spiritually rich worldview in which beliefs and traditions have evolved organically, where the cultural climate remains hostile but verdant. And the bruxa was the bringer of necessary interlocution between abundance and need. At least, until it was instrumentalized by authorities and used as a scapegoat for socio-political tensions. The existence of the *bruxa* presented a convenient motive for justifying the enforcement of Christian-derived spiritual development and morality. The first secular law against witchcraft passed in Europe was an edict from the 1424 *Ordinacions de les Valls d'Àneu* (Catalan Pyrenees). This law proposed the Pyrenees as one of the first epicentres for the late medieval and Early Modern witch hunt. By fusing the threat of *maleficium* born from an unseen menace with that of the already familiar *bruxa*, this law has been made responsible for the *bruxas'* conceptual transformation.

The law in question proclaimed the following:

> We firstly establish and command that from now on if any man or woman in the aforementioned valley [that is, the Valley of Àneu] is found to go at night with the bruxes to the Boc de Biterna, and pays homage to him, taking him as their lord, denying the name of God, and he or she kills or murders little children at day or night, and gives them gatirnons or buxols, and administers them metzines, such man or woman who commits those crimes shall lose their bodies; and their possessions (...) shall be confiscated by the lord.[1]

This edict catalogued a vast legacy of accumulated witch lore, and synthesised centuries of historiography with pre-existing local folklore. Once put into action, this legislature introduced a completely different alterity for the *bruxa*, one defined by its state of opposition to Christian society,[2] which conclusively influenced the socio-structural environment.

1 Transcription of the *Ordinacions de les Valls D'Àneu* in Padilla i Lafuente, J. J. 1999. *L'Esperit d'Àneu*. Esterri d'Àneu: Consell Cultural de les Valls d'Àneu. Translated by the author.
2 The *Ordinacions* law will be used throughout this book as a significant example of the crystallisation of the Pyrenean bruxa concept, when the primordial supernatural entity was given human attributes and linked with the already existing threat of heresy.

Direnik ez da sinistu bear; ez direla ez da esan bear
'YOU MUST NOT BELIEVE THAT THEY EXIST;
YOU CANNOT SAY THEY DO NOT EXIST'[3]

𝕬CCORDING to a legend from Ataun in Basque country, a group of spinners were walking down a road at night, talking about witches, and one of them claimed that witches did not exist. When they parted ways to return to their homes, the one who had made the claim encountered a group of witches who announced: 'We are not, yet we are, except from Maripetralín,[4] the rest are here'. Each witch took a hair from the doubtful spinner's head as punishment for her disbelief, and she ended up bald.[5]

What is this tale trying to convey? 'We are not, yet we are, except from Maripetralín, the rest are here'... is a strikingly ambiguous thing to say. Any interpretation, none of which can be definitive, must accommodate the idea of the Pyrenean witch being a liminal entity, whose existence is too taboo to acknowledge or even mention. The meaning of "we are not, yet we are" could mean both at once: that they are not of this world but that they do exist on another plane. Common folk must not actively *believe* that they exist, yet they should refrain from confirming their inexistence; yet, they cannot *say* that *bruxes* do not exist, lest they invite an encounter with, or an attack, from them. In a similarly vague manner, the *Ordinacions* law ruled against the men and women who went '*with the bruxes*', yet it never claimed that those men and women were *bruxes*, for bruxes were something else entirely. Similarly, the Basque phrase which provides the sub-title above aligns with that *ethos*, and is in fact present in a variety of local folktales

3 Old Basque saying about the existence of witches, present in several folktales, found in J. M. Barandiaran, *Brujería y brujas*. Donostia: Txertoa: (2012), 19.
4 Maripetralín probably refers to a popular witch from Basque folklore, protagonist of many tales.
5 Barandiaran, 19.

that make reference to the existence of *bruxes*.

By deciphering the etymology of the *bruxa*, some of the mysteries crucial for this investigation may be unveiled. The term *bruxa* is the natural antecedent to the old French *broux* (no longer in use), the Occitan *bruèisa*, *brèissa* or *broisha*, the Catalan *bruixa*, Spanish *bruja*, and Portuguese *bruxa*. Several academics have investigated its origin, although most of these studies are now obsolete. Nevertheless, it is important to highlight these early etymologies in order to see the symbolic implications that this word has been exposed to, as well as the paths that some scholars followed to uncover its source. Most modern researchers seem to agree on the Pyrenean origin of the word *bruxa*,[6] which would initially be linked with the action of crushing the chest or suffocating sleepers, same as the nightmare or the hag.

According to historian Pau Castell, the first occasion in which *bruxa* appeared in a written text was in the *Vocabulista in arabico*, a Catalan-Arabic dictionary written in 1257 by Ramon Martí, a Dominican friar. *Bruxa* was at the time translated into different Arabic terms including *qarîna*, and *kabûs*. This translation is key to understanding the term, since *qarîna* and *kabûs* make reference to night dwelling *succubi*-like entities, commonly feared due to their insatiable appetite for blood.[7] This translation of *bruxa* seems to support Castell's theory which claims the real origin for the term is to be found in the proto-Indo-European root *bhreus*: meaning 'to choke, to suffocate', an action which the dictionary author Ramon Martí attributed to supernatural entities who were feared for their vampiric actions against people in their sleep, and the abduction and killing of children.[8]

---

6 Fabián Alejandro Campagne, "Witch or Demon? Fairies, Vampires and Nightmares in Early Modern Spain." *Acta Ethnographica Hungarica. An International Journal of Ethnography* no. 53 (2008), 381–410; 392. Also Pau Castell, 'The Mythical Components of the Iberian Witch', *eHumanista n.s.* 26: (2014), 170–195, 171.

7 Ibid.

8 Castell, 'The Mythical Components of the Iberian Witch', 189. The asterisk (*) indicates that this is a reconstructed term.

For that reason, the most adequate translation for the bruxa would not entirely be that of witch, as it lacks the primordial component of other nocturnal entities like the ancient Roman *strix*, the Italian *strega*, the Romanian *strigoi*, the Greek *lamia*, the Germanic *hag*, or the nightmare. Like the aforementioned beings, the *bruxa* is an entity that dwells in the Underworld, not a Devil-worshipping or magic-performing human person. Conflated with faeries, demons, and the spirits of the Dead, the Pyrenean *bruxa* is a member of the spectral retinue, the one deemed responsible for granting wealth and boons to households as well as for nocturnal attacks. The presence of *bruxes* was an unquestioned reality among Pyrenean communities until the late medieval and Early Modern witch panic. Protection rituals, amulets, devotional offerings, and talismans were devised to keep them at bay, proven by innumerable examples present in Pyrenean households aimed at scaring *bruxes* and evil spirits away.[9]

The idea of the *bruxa* as a supernatural entity tallies with the Basque *sorgin* —*sorginak* in plural form. Same as it happened with *bruxa*, the *sorgin* was subject to a progressive humanization, to end up being used today as a synonym for a sorcerer or a diviner. The term *sorgin* appeared for the first time in the 13th century as part of the expression *Sorguinarizaga*, the 'oak tree forest of the sorgin'. It seems the term *sorgin* was originally used to designate a nocturnal entity that was connected to the Land and birth-making, as it can be seen by the parts that conform it: *sor-* 'to be born' and *-zain* 'to make or to take care'.[10] Basque folklorist and historian José Miguel de Barandiarán proposed the etymology could be linked with the action of threading fate, although it seems that etymological explanation would have been affected by the etymology of the French term *sorcier* (the antecessor of the English *sorcerer*), linked to the Latin *sortus* 'fate'. The primordial *sorgin* could have originally been

9 Olivier Marliave, *Dictionnaire de magie et de sorcellerie dans les Pyrénées*. Luçon: Éditions Sud-Ouest: (2006), 36–42.

10 Mikel Azurmendi, *Nombrar, embrujar. Para una historia del sometimiento de la cultura oral en el Paiís Vasco*. Irún: Aberdania, (1993), 243.

deemed as both a protective and a threatening spirit, able to affect the newly-born and their mothers, as well as being an integrative force in the making of the fate of human beings.[11] The Basque *sorgin* was thought of as a supernatural entity and servant of the Basque goddess Mari, a paramount deity in Basque cosmology, mistress of both the Land and the beyond. The connection to the goddess Mari has clear parallels to the European witch historiography, as the first religious accounts on primordial witches presented them as followers of the goddesses Diana or Herodias.[12] However, the relationship between *sorginak* and Mari, was only recently suggested in 20th-century texts.[13] Another possible etymology for the *sorgin*, and its first syllable *sor-*, could mean 'to stupefy, to numb someone', as this is found in the Basque verb *soreztatu*, 'to enchant or to bewitch'.[14] With all this, the etymology for *sorgin* seems to support a widespread belief in supernatural entities that had a definite influence in the daily life of Pyrenean communitiesOf course, this sort of belief in the existence of supernatural entities was not limited to the Pyrenean territories. Ancient Greek and Roman authors relate tales of the child-devouring *lamia* and the vampiric *strix*, fearful nocturnal creatures which established a precedent for the *bruxa*. The word lamia could also make reference to the *lemures*, the restless spirits of the dead from ancient times,[15] while *strix* refers to the action of shrieking attributed to those entities which, according to Ovid, drank the blood of infants and canni-

11 María Martínez Pisón. 'Etorkizuna, kontakizuna.' Por encima de todas las zarzas (September 2016). Available at: https://porencima-detodaslaszarzas.com/2016/09/29/etorkizuna-kontakizuna/ (Accessed 10 December 2019)
12 Julio Caro Baroja, *Las brujas y su mundo* (2006), 94-98.
13 Azurmendi, 241.
14 Ibid., 244.
15 Mallory, J. P. Mallory and Douglas Adams, *Encyclopedia of Indo-European Culture*. London: Fitzroy Dearborn Publishers, 1989. Available at: <https://archive.org/details/EncyclopediaOfIndoEuropeanCulture/> p. 583 [Accessed 10 March 2020]

balized people.[16] The 6th century law known as *Lex Salica* attested the belief in the existence of *strigae* in Germanic territories, and proposed a series of punishments against them.[17] Nevertheless, *strigae* were not seen as terrifying night birds capable of attacking people, instead they were thought of as anthropophagic entities that roamed the Land at night, frightening people in their sleep. The fearsome, cannibalistic, and vampiric features attributed to *strigae* parallel the noxious deeds attributed to the *bruxa*.

Linking *strigae* and the *bruxa* to cannibalism, especially infanticide, positions both as deviations from the laws of nature,[18] reaffirmed by persistent accusations against certain portions of the population considered deviant. In Roman antiquity, Christian communities were accused of killing children and carrying out orgies. The same indictment resurfaced as part of the accusations for identifying heretical sects in the Middle Ages.[19] Charges of cannibalism and infanticide imposed onto *bruxes* and individuals who followed them could be considered as merely justification for the fears of the religious elites and other authorities, but they could also be taken as evidence of trance journeying or detachment of the Spirit Double, a manifestation of one or many parts of the human self or *alter ego*, which detaches itself during trance, dreams, and in death. According to anthropologist Emma Wilby, cannibalism and infanticide were attributed to those who could go with spirits or access the spirit world.[20] In this sense, the Pyrenean *bruxa* would not only be a supernatural entity, but also a state of non-being which some individuals are able to achieve.

Such a possibility was not new, but was previously noted in Regino of Prüm's *Canon Episcopi*, written in the 10th century:

16 Ovidio. 2001. *Fastos* (2001), 207–208.

17 Norman Cohn, *Los Demonios Familiares de Europa* (1976), 265–266.

18 Carlo Ginzburg, *Ecstasies. Deciphering The Witches' Sabbath* (1989), 74.

19 Cohn, *Los Demonios Familiares de Europa*, 12.

20 This thesis is explored by Emma Wilby in "Burchard's strigae, the Witches' Sabbath, and Shamanistic Cannibalism in Early Modern Europe." *Magic, Ritual, and Witchcraft*, 18–48.

It is also not to be omitted that some wicked women, turning back to Satan, seduced by illusions and phantasms of demons, believe and claim that in the hours of night, they ride on certain beasts with Diana, goddess of the pagans, and an innumerable multitude of women; they are called to her service on particular nights, and in the dismal silence of the night, traverse great spaces of earth and obey her commends as mistress. (...) and although it is only her spirits that endures this, the faithless mind thinks that it happens not in the spirit but in the body. Who indeed has not been led out of himself in dreams and nocturnal visions and sees many things while sleeping which he had never seen while awake? Who indeed is so stupid and dull that they think that there things occur in the body that happen in the spirits (...)? [21]

To which bishop Burchard of Worms would add interesting specifications in his canonical text *Corrector sive medicus*, written less than a hundred years later:

Have you believed what many women who have turned back to Satan believe and affirm to be true, namely, that in the quiet of the night when you go to bed with your husband laying next to you, you are able to go out through the closed doors and traverse vast the spaces of the world with many others who are deceived by a similar error, and that without visible arms can kill people who have been baptised and redeemed by the blood of Christ in order to eat their cooked flesh, and in place of their heart to put something like straw or wood, and once they are eaten you can make them live again for another interval of life. If you have believed this, you must do penance for 40 days (...) [22]

---

21 Regino of Prüm, "Synodal Cases and Church Discipline". In Martha Rampton, *European Magic and Witchcraft: A Reader*, 155.
22 Burchard of Worms, *Decretum* (2018), 156.

From these texts rises a theological concern caused by a widespread belief in retinues of nocturnal entities which were deemed responsible for carrying out nocturnal attacks, as well as the possibility for some individuals to accompany them in something that, we are repeated again and again, was not a physical travel, but a flight of the spirit. Engaging in out-of-body-experiences or spirit flight has often been categorised as a shamanistic trait. It can also be presumed that the primary role of the supernatural night cannibal was not entirely evil, as they could receive payment for protection and good fortune. Offerings of food, sleep disturbances, or even the abduction and killing of cattle and people, especially children, could be regarded as a payment in exchange for protection. According to the *Ordinacions*, the first European civil law on witchcraft, people could join the *bruxes* or even become one of them and engage in such actions. The conditions for going with the *bruxes* shall be examined in the fifth chapter.

Before the publication of the *Canon Episcopi* in the 10th century, human interaction with intangible spirits was deemed possible by theological elites, and the existence of supernatural and demonic entities was a widely accepted reality among the highest religious spheres. The *Canon* fought to change this perception, and belief in the supernatural was turned into an 'infidelity'. Holding those beliefs would soon become a sign of Devil worship and paganism for religious authorities such as Regino of Prüm and Burchard of Worms. Accordingly, the law ratified a discursive shift and urged local religious authorities to inform about that same shift to whoever concurred with this new rendition of folkloric practices:

> Therefore, priests throughout their churches are required to pronounce this crime to the people, with all insistence, so this will be known to be lies in every way...[23]

After the 14th century, contact with demonic spirits and the Devil was believed to allow people to enact their deepest desires and de-

---

23 Cohn, *Los Demonios Familiares de Europa*, 269.

stroy everyday restrictions by shaking off the constraints imposed by moral edicts. This principle endured for centuries in mountain communities, exemplified by the perspective of Benito Feijóo, a 17th century Benedictine monk, who proposed that demons and spirits allowed the individual to:

> commit as many crimes as he feels like. He can kill, take away honour, steal, burn down villages, (...) he knows no one can touch a hair of his head because all is cloaked with the imagination that the devil did it all.[24]

What had once been regarded as a superstition between the 10th and 15th centuries—that is, between the *Canon Episcopi* and the *Ordinacions*—was now re-established as an actual threat to society, and would remain so until the Enlightenment. This change in the symbolic order could indeed be seen as one of the most destructive perceptual shifts in western culture. Quoting Italian philosopher Luisa Muraro:

> The witch-hunt effectually begins with a collapse of boundaries between fantasy and reality: from the repression of the medieval beliefs in the nocturnal flights of witches and other similar beliefs, we move on to the 14th and 15th century legal persecution of women and men (majority of women, though) who were accused of fantastic crimes which had, until then, been regarded as delusive fantasies inspired by the Evil One, as the venerable Canon episcopi recited [...] The witch-hunt can be seen as a catastrophic loss of the boundaries between fantasy and reality, and as an individual and collective commitment to build yet another boundary. Or, to put it more simply, it could be regarded as a change in the symbolic order. [...] I think that was the actual birth of

---

24 Emma Wilby. 'Burchard's strigae, the Witches' Sabbath, and Shamanistic Cannibalism in Early Modern Europe': *Magic, Ritual, and Witchcraft*.

modern civilisation. From the struggle to affirm faith in the true God (understood not in a fideistic way, but as a guarantee of a sense of reality) against the delusions inspired by the evil spirit (equated with mental delirium), which was the position of the medieval Church, we move on to the repression of certain beliefs, understood in a realistic way (...) [25]

When the ideas of the Enlightenment started emerging, the ancient and medieval certainty on the existence of *bruxes* and the possibility of joining them was classified as an ignorant superstition. But let us elaborate on that concept. Superstition, which derives from the Latin *super stare* 'stand over', refers to beliefs apart from the normalised or established religion, and therefore indicative of sin. A Navarrese theologian, Martin of Arles, strongly advised against superstitions in the late 15th century in his *Tractatus de superstitionibus, contra maleficia seu sortilegia quae hodie vigent in orbe terrarum.* His thoughts on superstition not only limited belief in the supernatural but also pre-Christian customs, for example, using bells to ward off bad weather, or the use of amulets and talismans, which he regarded as *nonsensical absurdities from the ancient times.*[26] This systematic prosecution of heterodox pseudo-religious ideas suggests the rapidly growing distance between religious elites and common folk. Despite any prohibitions, many supposedly superstitious customs, beliefs and "nonsensical absurdities" remained widely prevalent, particularly in rural communities where *bruxes* continued to be feared.

Laws and recommendations intended to regulate superstitions tended to fail, likely due to the common people's reluctance to deny the existence of other-than-human entities. Its persistence is evident in the first trial of a person accused of going with the *bruxes*: Sança de Camins, a 30-year-old woman, tried in Barce-

---

25 "Ir libremente entre sueño y realidad" in *Acta historica et archaeologica mediaevalia*, no. 19, 364-374; 365-369.

26 Mikel Azurmendi, 'A Vueltas Con El Término Akelarre' (2012), 42–53, 49.

lona in 1419. Sança was a reputed midwife skilled in delivering babies and protecting mothers and children from harm during childbirth. When put to trial, she was asked "whether she had ever gone with those women called *bruxes*",[27] and she was accused of gathering with *bruxes* and attacking new-born children. Sança defended herself, denying these crimes by explaining that the protection rituals she performed were in fact designed to prevent *bruxes* and the *Trip* from attacking children and their mothers, not the other way around.

The *Trip* mentioned in Sança's trial has been mistakenly identified by some researchers as a representation of the Triple Goddess.[28] Other historians have more accurately traced it back to an expression similar to 'Royal Tribe', a concept analogous to the Wild Hunt, the *Unholden*, the *Malandanti*, or the Elf Court, all being the hellish cavalcade of supernatural spirits who roamed the countryside.[29] The protection or offering ritual in the testimony of Sança involved preparing a table by laying a tablecloth, whereupon wine, bread, water and a mirror were placed. The *Trip* would then appear and become so distracted by glimpses of their reflections in the mirror, along with the offering of food and drink, that they were unable to hurt the baby or mother. The trial transcription states:

> That she often set the table at night with food and a tablecloth and bread and wine and water and a mirror, so that those of the Trip would look into it and trouble themselves eating and drinking and looking themselves in the mirror, and thus they wouldn't attack the little children. [...] And so in this manner the child would be delivered, that there

27 Pau Castell, 'The Mythical Components of the Iberian Witch' (2014), 173.

28 Teresa Vinyoles Vidal, 'Llevadores, guaridores i fetilleres. Exemples de sabers i pràctiques femenines a la Catalunya medieval' (2013–2014), 23–32, 22.

29 Castell, 'The Mythical Components of the Iberian Witch', 175.

would be no need to fear for the Trip.[30]

It seemed that Sança set an altar to appease the *bruxes* by distracting their attention from the baby and, with the available evidence, that this interaction was related to propitiation rites. This protective ceremony resembles practices performed in honour of Frau Holda or Perchta in Germanic lands, deities associated with the supernatural retinue of entities that scared the living, and to whom people left offerings of food and drink in order to spare their lives or their harvests.[31]

The idea behind some specific deities being leaders of an infernal cavalcade is also featured in Pyrenean folklore; a deity or spirit known as Bensozia in the French Pyrenees,[32] is referred to as the leader of the *bonnes dames* or *bones dones*, the 'good ladies'.[33] Bensozia itself seems to be a corruption of the expression *bona socia*, 'the good partner', an euphemistic expression employed to seek the beneficial disposition of those entities. Bensozia was first mentioned in the *Statuts synodaux* written by Auger II de Montfaucon, bishop of Couserans (French Pyrenees) in the 13th century, and was described as the leader of a retinue of spirits, including witches and the spirits of the dead, as well as a 'multitude of women.' [34] Of course, the Basque goddess Mari also comes to mind; also known as the Lady, she was believed to be a deity that controlled weather and commanded storms. Depicted as a ruler of life and death over all living things, she was bestowed with the

---

30 Josep Hernando, 'Processos inquisitorials per crim d'heretgia i una apel·lació per maltractament i parcialitat per part de l'inquisidor (1440) Documents dels protocols notarials', (2005), 75-104; in Castell 2014, 175.

31 Cohn, *Los Demonios Familiares de Europa*, 273.

32 Ginzburg, *Ecstasies*, 91.

33 Fabián Alejandro Campagne, 'Witch or Demon? Fairies, Vampires and Nightmares in Early Modern Spain' (2008), 381-410, 391.

34 Carabia Jacqueline. "Christianisation superficielle dans la région de Lannemezan." (2001). Paris: Editions du CTHS (2002). 65-77. (Actes du Congrès national des sociétés savantes, 126).

responsibility of leading the cavalcades of the *sorginak*, the *bruxes*. Her masks included a beautiful woman, a he-goat, a bird-footed woman, a raven, and a vulture; a shape reminiscent of the Roman *strix*.[35] Her attributes parallel other European pre-Christian goddesses in charge of the Night Host and spirits of the Underworld. What makes Mari unique is that her role is still recognised in a variety of folk customs and beliefs in several Basque communities.

'CAUSERS OF MISCHIEF AND DEATH': THE *BRUXA* IS HUMANISED

ℝELIGIOUS and moral authorities would progressively transform the primordial supernatural *bruxa* into a human representative of transgression, prompting the large-scale prosecution we now know as the witch hunt. Such a structural change would imply that other segments of society were attributed with supernatural abilities. Explicit links between *bruxa* and *maleficium* did not appear in written texts until the 13th century, although magical and heterodox practices had been prosecuted since ancient times. Laws regarding harmful sorcery or *maleficium*, such as the *Codex Teodosianus,* appeared in Europe from the 5th century onwards, against those who conjured storms, invoked demons, and performed blood sacrifices.[36] In the region of Languedoc,[37] records of prohibition against sorcerers and diviners appear as early as the 6th century.

Torcimany, a lexicon written in the 14th century by the Catalan poet Lluís d'Aversó, shows proof of the gradual humanisation of the *bruxa* by giving two entries for the word: one meaning *per la fentasme* 'for the phantasm', making reference to the supernatural entity, and another meaning: *per lo bruxar,* 'for the sorcery', referring to the sorcerous act of *maleficium*.[38] While supernatural

---

35 Barandiaran, J.M. *Mitología Vasca.* (2001), 86-88.
36 Caro Baroja, *Las brujas y su mundo,* 75.
37 Cohn, *Los Demonios Familiares de Europa*, 205.
38 Castell, 'The Mythical Components of the Iberian Witch', 172.

entities were believed to be naturally inclined to perpetuate harm, people who went with the *bruxes* were thought to do so with the help of *maleficium* and their allegiance to the Devil, and under this guise they dedicated themselves to sullying the three pillars associated with mountain and rural community life: human and animal well-being, and weather. The *bruxa* would progressively lose its supernatural appeal in front of flesh and bone threats to society, embodied by healers and connoisseurs of sorcery and magic.

In the *Ordinacions*, which provides a rounded view of the facets that form the *bruxa*, people who were said to accompany them were attributed with the ability to perform actions that had traditionally been ascribed only to supernatural entities:

> ...and he or she kills or murders little infants at day or night, and gives them gatirnons or buxols, and administers them metzines, that such man or woman who commits those crimes shall lose their bodies; and their possessions ...shall be confiscated by the lord.[39]

This declaration allowed '*bruxa*' to be used as an umbrella term for identifying supernatural spirits and the individuals capable of committing *maleficium* or harmful magic. It refers to the giving of *gatirnons*; goiters, *buxols*; a poison most probably linked to the plant *Anemone nemorosa*, and administration of *metzines;* a term used to refer to both medicines and poisons.

Maleficium affected the health of people, their ability to procreate, caused irremediable maladies, and affected the health of cattle, particularly the quality of their milk and meat, along with the survival of the youngest animals. Moreover, *maleficium* affected the fertility of the harvest and daily life by producing inclement weather.[40] Pyrenean *bruxes* were also linked to the conjuration of

---

39 Transcription of the *Ordinacions de les Valls D'Àneu* in J. J. Padilla i Lafuente, *L'Esperit d'Àneu* (1999). Translated by the author.

40 It is interesting to note that the idea of maleficium affecting weather is as ancient as the 6th century, when Visigoths spoke of the tempes-

bad weather and disastrous storms, for such reasons we can still find simple constructions called *comunidors* (also known as *conjuratories* in French, or *exconjuraderos* in Spanish) in the Pyrenees today.[41] *Comunidors* are small constructions typically placed in fields or next to a church, and are used as a platform for priests and folk healers to scare off storms, by reciting exorcism prayers while at the same time wielding iron knives against menacing clouds. Mikel Azurmendi, a Basque anthropologist, highlighted the threat *maleficium* posed, and the capacity of some individuals to perform it regardless of their faith or lack thereof during the Middle Ages:

> Did the common people believe in witches in the same way in which they believed in God, Heaven and Hell (...)? I'm afraid not: farmer communities experienced maleficium as something that dictated their daily lives and gave meaning to the invisible-intangible things in their world. The idea of maleficium probably was part of the corpus of "common sense" truths and assumptions, which are the only ground in which people build their perceptions, experiences, certainties, discourses, predictions, and efficient results.[42]

A letter dated 1023, written by the bishop Oliva from Vic to Sancho el Mayor, King of Pamplona (Navarra), gave the first signs of concern regarding the use of *maleficium* and sorcery in the Pyrenees. In the epistle, the clergyman advises the monarch to take care of the increasing number of foreigners and augurs in their lands. Historian and folklorist Ángel Gari Lacruz states, the mentioning of augurs conflated divination practices with *maleficia*. This intervention by the bishop in this letter to the King indicates that the problem had spread beyond measure.[43] It would be another two

---

tarii, a series of sorcerers who could conjure storms by splashing water, or hitting the water with sticks, or throwing stones at water.

41 Marliave, *Dictionnaire de magie et de sorcellerie dans les Pyrénées*, 103–104.
42 Azurmendi, 'A Vueltas Con El Término Akelarre', 42–53, 49.
43 Angel Gari Lacruz, Ángel, 'Brujería en Aragon' (1981), 27.

hundred years until the first law against sorcery was passed in the Pyrenees of Aragon, as attested by its presence in the *In Excelsis Dei Thesauris,* a compilation of legal and religious texts redacted between 1247 and 1252 by the bishop of Huesca, Vidal de Canellas. In the text, the bishop supported the prosecution of all sorcerers and poison makers, called posouers or metziners: "ueneficus, or those who give pozones (poisons) must receive death if what they do results in the death of a victim. If the victim does not die, the victim must do whatever they want with the individual who gave the poisons."[44]

The law spread onto other Pyrenean lands, as the first trials against individuals concerning magic would primarily involve the crime of *veneficium*, known in the Pyrenees as *ponzoñería/ metzineria*, i.e. poison-making. The impact that this text had on society is demonstrated by observing the shift in the meaning of the word *metzina*: from designating both good and harmful medicine to exclusively denoting poison. Shortly thereafter, *maleficium*, sorcery, and ceremonial magic were amalgamated into the intangible crime of witchcraft. The new *bruxa*, now in humanised form, was enriched with the abilities and crafts of the sorcerer and sorceress, the diviner, the folk healer, and the poisoner. *Bruxes* were now undeniably human, and capable of magical actions with the help of Satan. *Maleficium* and the *bruxa* would henceforth be interpreted in a new light, for the supernatural entity had become a tool used by the Devil to spread his dominion over earth.

'THOSE WHO HAVE IT, SHALL KEEP IT':
PROSECUTION AGAINST DEVIL-WORSHIPPERS AND HERETICS

THE final section of the *Ordinacions* analysed in this chapter pertains to the Pyrenean *bruxes* and the people who joined them in their night rides paying homage to the *Boc de Biterna,* the 'billy-goat of Biterna'—in other words, the Devil. Followers of the *bruxa*

---

44 Gunnar Tilander, and Vidal Mayor, *Traducción aragonesa de la obra In Excelsis Dei Thesauris de Vidal de Canellas* (1956), 499.

did not limit themselves to committing *maleficium* and *metzineria*, they also took the Devil *as their lord*, that is, they willingly followed him in their orgiastic ceremonies and *denied the name of God*.[45]

Heresy was already a well-established crime across Europe during the Middle Ages, and the Pyrenees was no exception to this phenomenon. Acts of heresy included the celebration of orgies, blood sacrifice, vampirism, infanticide, and incest. The bull known as *Vox in rama*, sent by Pope Gregory IX in 1233, established the parameters of heretical rituals, which consisted of kissing toads, the presence of pale or cold-skinned men or black cats, orgies, and making any offenses against God, such as spitting or stomping on crosses.[46] What probably started as a narrative for serving the interests of the religious elite became a campaign to exuviate the remnants of deviant immoral behaviour.

The Pyrenean connection between heresy and the new crime of witchcraft can be attributed to the Waldensians, an ascetic sect from the 12th century founded in Lyon, France. Although the Waldensians were excommunicated in 1184, their influence and ideas rapidly spread from France to Aragon and Catalonia through the Pyrenees. Members of the sect were accused of celebrating orgies in caves, such reunions were apparently presided over by the Devil in the shape of an infernal dragon, whereupon they allegedly articulated their goal and made pacts to destroy Christianity.[47] In their trials, Waldensian preachers, called *barbes*, claimed masses ended with the phrase: 'those who have it shall keep it', referring to the symbolic and allegorical meaning of the attendees as receptors of a mystical secret, after which they would turn the lights out and meditate in the dark.[48] The cathartic ending to the Waldensian mass would later be incorporated to the Pyrenean witches' sabbat or *ajunt de bruxes*.

45 J. J. Padilla i Lafuente, J. J., *L'Esperit d'Àneu*. Esterri d'Àneu: Consell Cultural de les Valls d'Àneu (1999). Translated by the author.
46 Cohn, *Los Demonios Familiares de Europa*, 53.
47 Ibid., 55–63.
48 Ibid., 66.

In the French text, *Le champion des dames*, written by Martin
Le France in 1451, and the *Traité du crisme de vauderie*, written by
the Belgian Johannes Tinctoris circa 1470, Waldensians are presented as having contact with demons. They were thought capable
of flying through the air and celebrating devilish ceremonies to
please their master. In fact, for some time, *bruxes* in France were
categorised as *nouveau vaudois,* the 'new Waldensians'.[49] Thus, the
bruxa eventually became a Devil worshipper, a link that was facili-
tated by pre-existing folk beliefs about the Devil, which will be
explored in the next chapter. The new bruxa, heretical and maleficent, did not only provoke fear in the common people, who protected their ways of living from an invisible but familiar menace,
but it was also frightening to the elites, as it linked disobedience
with a threat to power.

The idea of *bruxes* and heretics as being threats to power culminated with the French judge Pierre de Lancre, who was responsible for the infamous large-scale *auto de fé* and witch trial in 1610
in Logroño (Basque Country). De Lancre, using his experiences in
the Basque Country and Navarra to write the famous treaty *Tableau de l'inconstance des mauvais anges et demons,* is considered a pivotal source in understanding Pyrenean witchcraft. Judge De Lancre claimed that Basque people were naturally inclined to practice
witchcraft because of their inconsistent weather, their complicated
political system, and the broad division of power in their church.[50]
De Lancre claimed *bruxes* should be considered natural-born trai-
tors to power, thus making a diabolic pact a political crime, with
bruxes being tried as *criminals against divine majesty.*[51]

The crime of witchcraft eventually affected all strata of society,
and the idea of the *bruxa* being a threat to the established system

49 Pau Castell, *Orígens i evolució de la cacera de bruixes a Catalunya* (2013). Available at: <http://diposit.ub.edu/dspace/bit-
stream/2445/51863/1/01.PCG_1de2.pdf> p. 83 [Accessed 12 December 2019]
50 Caro Baroja, *Las brujas y su mundo,* 210.
51 Azurmendi, Mikel. *Nombrar, embrujar,* 234.

continued to retain its relevance throughout the centuries. Karl
Ernst Jarcke claimed in 1828 that practitioners of witchcraft were
a clandestine anti-Christian movement who willingly followed a
pre-Christian religion, a theory later adopted by Margaret Murray
in her witch-cult hypothesis.[52] Jules Michelet, another 19th century French historian whose theories have been recently refuted,
understood witchcraft to be a device employed by the oppressed,
claiming that witchcraft was a tool for women and peasantry to
regain their lost power. As it can be seen, the other-than-human
primordial aspects of the *bruxa* had been now completely set aside.

'GOOD IT IS THAT THERE ARE HERETICS, SO THOSE WHO ARE
STRAIGHT AND APPROVED BY FAITH WILL BE KNOWN':[53]
WITCH-TRIALS IN THE PYRENEES

THE Pyrenean witch craze started much earlier than in other
European areas, this can be attributed to the early prosecutions of heretic groups, *magi*, and *maleficii*.[54] Before even bruxes
were even part of the equation, there were outbursts of prosecution against magic in Pyrenean territories, like those motivated by
Pyrenean-born bishop Jacques Fournier, who would later become
pope Benedict XII in 1319. Before becoming pope, Fournier carried out an exhaustive investigation on the matter of heresy in
the village of Montaillou (French Pyrenees). In the course of his
investigations, Fournier interrogated an interesting character, that
of assistant sacristan Arnaud Gélis, an *armier* 'messenger of souls'
who had witnessed infernal hunts and delivered messages from
the dead to the living.[55] Fournier's predecessor in the papal role,
John XII, who lived in the French Pyrenees for some time, was the

52 Cohn, *Los Demonios Familiares de Europa*, 142
53 Attributed to Saint Paul. Caro Baroja, Julio, *Brujería Vasca*, 52.
54 Franco Cardini, *Magia, stregoneria, superstizioni nell'Occidente medievale*
(1972), 73-74.
55 Le Roy Ladurie, *Montaillou: The Promised Land of Error*. First published in 1978.

main instigator of the papal bull *Super illius specula* in 1326, which deemed all witches heretics. From then on, witchcraft could be tried by the inquisition. He conducted a couple of inquisitorial tests in the French Pyrenean towns of Toulouse and Carcassonne against people accused of practicing magic and sorcery between 1320 and 1330.[56]

Still, the folkloric component of the bruxa could not be entirely shaken off by local authorities. Thus, the first cases against alleged *bruxes* focused on prosecuting individuals that carried out criminal actions against their community, bearing a strong resemblance with actions attributed to supernatural *bruxes*. In 1471, in the region of Urgell (Catalan Pyrenees), the accused Guillema Casala declared herself guilty of going with the *bruxes* to break into houses at night, and of *bruxar*, or 'crushing' a child.[57] The action of *bruxar*, crushing the chest of a sleeping person, corresponds to the prototypical actions attributed to the cannibalistic and infanticidal *bruxa* (a deeper analysis of actions attributed to those who claimed to go with the *bruxes* will be established in the fifth chapter). In 1551, the territories of Andorra witnessed the trial of Antònia Martina, accused of causing illnesses and poison making. Accusations rapidly increased to over twenty individuals from neighbouring villages, and even though they were charged with Devil-worshipping rituals and committing heresy, the word *lamia* was still used in written accounts to refer to the accused, a sign of the prevalence of the primordial idea of the *bruxa*. Unfortunately, the outcome for the trial has been lost, even though it is considered one of the most relevant witch trials in the Principality.[58]

The *bruxa* was progressively transformed into a tangible threat to the lives of the community, steadily moving from a distant supernatural danger to a closer and more tangible menace. *Metzineria* and *fetilleria* (poison making and sorcery) were often regarded as

---

56 Jeffrey Burton Russell, *Witchcraft in the Middle Ages* (1984), 144.
57 Castell, 'The Mythical Components of the Iberian Witch', 170-195, 189.
58 Robert Pastor i Castillo, *Aquí les penjaven* (2004), 170-173.

the tools of those accused as *bruxes* or of practising witchcraft to cause misfortune. Poison-making's relevance in Pyrenean witch-craft began in Navarra[59] and France,[60] but arguably the most representative case took place in the Aragonese Pyrenees in the late 15th century: the trial of Guirandana De Lay. She lived in the principality of Villanúa, although her surname's origin suggests she may have been born in the French territory of Béarn.[61] If so, her provenance merits closer attention, as more than thirty people in that area were tried for metzineria between 1390 and 1510.[62] People likely fled the region to avoid facing similar indictments; perhaps Guirandana was among them.[63] She was accused along with her mother Vicienta of being a *pessima, homicida, fetillera,* and *poçonera:* 'bad woman, homicidal, sorceress, and poisoner'. The poisons she was accused of manufacturing with her alleged accomplices were made from animal and human remains, mandrake, and henbane.[64] Even though Guirandana was never accused of being a *bruxa,* the case marked a precedent in Aragon, as it sparked the creation of a royal ordinance to deal with similar cases, and marked the art of poison-making as a sign of witchcraft.

59 In 1279, the first legal prosecution was brought against a woman from Navarra who was accused of administering herbal remedies. José Antonio Fernández Otal, 'Guirandana de Lay, hechicera, ¿bruja? y ponzoñera de Villanúa (Alto Aragon), según un proceso criminal del año 1461' (2006), 35-172; 157.

60 In 1328, the first French detentions were reported, starting with the procedure carried against Johana la Christiana from Bidache (living in the French region of Aquitaine, next to Navarra), who *empozonaba la gent et era herbolera mala,* ('gave poisons and was a bad herbalist'). Nicolas Ghersi, 'Poisons, sorcières et lande de bouc' (2009) Available at: <http://journals.openedition.org/crm/11496> [Accessed: 12 December 2019], 103-120, 106.

61 Fernández Otal, 'Guirandana de Lay, hechicera, ¿bruja? y ponzoñera de Villanúa (Alto Aragon), según un proceso criminal del año 1461'; 139.

62 Ibid., 163.

63 Ibid.,139.

64 Ibid.,142.

The practice of sorcery, *fetilleria*, became another common accusation in Pyrenean witch trials. The French historian Nicolas
Ghersi suggests that these sorts of crimes were not limited to the
lower strata of society, but were also practised by the ruling class,[65]
supported by the trial of the Countess of Urritzaga, who was convicted of making fetishes and condemned to die at the stake in
1338. The same accusation and fate was shared by the Countess of
Beheytie, together with two other women in 1370.[66] In early trials (before the 15th century), the accused were often referred to
as fetillers, and the mention of the *bruxa* was often put aside; in
the 15th and 16th century trials, magicians, fetillers, and metziners
are referred to as *bruxes*. A relevant example is found in the case
against Pere l'Hereu, from the Cóma de Mont-rós, 1548, accused of
being a 'bruyxot'—male *bruxa*—and said to have used corpses for
the making of metzines and poisoning people.[67]

Judicial practices seem to flow in parallel to the conceptual evolution of the *bruxa*. Trials against individuals accused of supernatural actions began to disappear in favour of judicial processes
where groups of people were accused of being *bruxes* and worshipping the Devil. Trials against Devil-worshipping conspiracies
started with the case against Valentina Guarner. She was tried in
the location of Pont de Suert, in the Catalan Pyrenees in 1484, only
sixty years after the *Ordinacions*. In her trial, she admitted to having been initiated into a coven of *bruxes* by two men, and claimed
that after anointing herself with a magical salve she would fly to
the *Lana del Boc*, 'Land of the Goat', where she would see the Boc
de Biterna, the Devil.[68]

The first large-scale witch trial in the Pyrenees was against the
Durangas of Amboto, in the Basque country in 1507.[69] 'Duranga'

65 Ghersi, 'Poisons, sorcières et lande de bouc', 107.
66 Ibid., 107.
67 Castell, *Orígens i evolució de la cacera de bruixes a Catalunya*, 233–248.
68 José Lladonosa Pujol, *El cas singular de na Valentina Guarner del Anecdotari de l'Estudi General de Lleida* (1988), 105–106.
69 Discredited historian Lamothe Langon claimed that the first large-
scale witch trial took place in Carcassonne and Toulouse (French

indicated their origin in the Basque city of Durango, but from the trial onwards it became synonymous with *sorgin* or *bruxa*. Accused of belonging to a sect that worshipped Beelzebub, *Durangas* were believed to have committed *maleficium* against people and cattle.[70] However, the case of the *Durangas* is unique, since the cave of Amboto, the purported dwelling of the accused, was and still is believed to be one of the homes of the goddess Mari.[71] There is further evidence of similar trials occurring in the area of Guipuzcoa and Biscaya in 1527, 1555, and 1575,[72] all of which were placed under the auspices of the Inquisition.[73] A retrospective account of the period confirms an extended witchcraft problem in the territory before the famous prosecution in Logroño (1610).[74] [75]

The Pyrenean witch panic reached its peak at the dawn of the 17th century, with the areas of Navarra and Catalonia as their epicentre. In Navarra, the crisis culminated in the *auto de fé*[76] of Logroño and the trials of Zugarramurdi and Hondarribia in 1610, and the death of eleven people.[77] Luckily, the mass hysteria was soon extinguished by figures like Alonso de Salazar y Frías, a mem-

---

Pyrenees) between 1320 and 1350, in which 400 people were tried and 200 were executed. This fact, however, is still in question. Jacques Dubourg, *Historie des sorcières et sorciers dans le Sud-Ouest* (2013), 17.

70 Caro Baroja, *Brujería Vasca*, 13.
71 For further reading see Iñaki Bazán, 'Superstición y brujería en el Duranguesado a fines de la Edad Media: ¿Amboto 1507?' (2011), 202/224.
72 Caro Baroja, *Brujería Vasca*, 25-69.
73 Carlos Rilova Jericó, 'Las últimas brujas de Europa - Acusaciones de brujería en el País Vasco' (2002) 363-393, 371.
74 Ángel Gari Lacruz, 'La brujería en los Pirineos (siglos XIII al XVII) Aproximación a su historia' (2010) 317-354, 338.
75 In the French Pyrenees, large-scale witch trials linked sorcery to the arrival of the plague, like the one that took place in Toulouse in 1535, where sixty-three men and women were tried. Dubourg (2013), 21.
76 An *auto de fe* is a public event in which those accused by the inquisition abjure their sins and show repentance.
77 Jesús María Usunáriz Garayoa. 'La caza de brujas en la Navarra moderna (siglos XVI-XVII)' 2012, 306-350, 316.

ber of the Inquisition whose independent point of view prevented further indictments from reaching a critical stage. He advised great caution and discretion when dealing with such matters in order to avoid creating further social alarm.[78] The magnitude of the Zugarramurdi case marked a change in the Inquisition's approach, which for most cases adopted an indifference towards witch trials, and only thanks to the intervention of individuals such as Salazar, began applying a more tolerant approach towards such accusations.[79]

The territories of Catalonia were not overtaken by the number of prosecutions reached in the Navarra region, however historians like Agustí Alcoberro claim that at least four hundred documented executions took place between 1617 and 1622.[80] It is no surprise to learn that prosecutions peaked in 1617, a year which is known as *Lo Any del Diluvi*, 'The Year of the Deluge', referring to a lengthy episode of low temperatures and terrible rain storms which caused illnesses in people and cattle.[81] Despite the fame attributed to the Inquisition and its torture methods, its role in Catalonia between 1617 and 1622 was that of a moderating and conciliatory agent, quite different from the position it had acquired in the campaigns of Navarra and the Basque Country.[82]

In Catalonia, civil tribunals were responsible for administering justice in witch trials, along with corresponding interrogations and methods of torture. During the height of the witch panic, in the 1620s, there appeared Pere Gil, known as *Defensor de les bruxes*, 'Defender of witches'; perhaps he might be considered the Catalan equivalent to Alonso de Salazar. Gil, also an Inquisition consultant,

---

78 Carmelo Lisón Tolosana, 1992. *Las brujas en la historia de España*. Madrid: Temas de Hoy: pp. 152-156.
79 For further reading see Gustav Henningsen, *The Witches' Advocate: Basque Witchcraft and the Spanish Inquisition*. Reno: Nevada University Press, 1980.
80 Agustí Alcoberro. *El segle de les bruixes*, (1992), 120.
81 Agustí Alcoberro. 'Cacera de bruixes, justícia local i Inquisició. a Catalunya, 1487-1643: alguns criteris metodològics' (2008), 485-504, 503.
82 Ibid.

decided to put an end to the abuses committed in trials by recommending that:

> It should be proceeded with caution and maturity regarding witches, because it seems, and it may be true, that some of them are innocent; and if some are guilty, as they are blind and fooled by the Devil because of their damnation and ill-doings, most of them do not deserve death penalty.[83]

The Supreme Court of Catalonia would eventually appeal most of the prosecutions in 1622 from civil tribunals, and once all the responsibilities were taken over, most of the accused were freed.[84] This marked the beginning of the end of the Catalan witch hunts.[85]

In Aragon, unlike the rest of the Pyrenees, trials were conducted under the auspices of Royal assent, meaning that *bruxes* could be immediately tried and executed without appeal.[86] Prosecutions started later than in other territories, notably in the last decade of the 16th century. One prosecution in the region of Alta Ribagorza executed twenty-two women in less than a month.[87] What is particularly interesting is that while the witch panic had subsided across Pyrenean territories, the Aragonese pursuit of *bruxes* persisted unabated, even if those accused faced less severe punishments.[88] The decreasing gravity of the trials is exemplified in the case of Agueda Cisneros, charged with being a *bruja* and *hechicera* in 1642. She was widely known for her magic and even admitted having performed beneficial spells, one of which involved captur-

83 *Memorial que el padre Pedro Gil, rector del Collegio de los jesuitas, dio al duque de Alburquerque en defensa de las bruxas el año de 1619. Con unas respuestas de un doctor en leyes de la villa de Perpiñán,* in Alcoberro (2007), 140-156, 143. (translated by author)
84 Ibid., 140-156.
85 Ibid., 148.
86 Gari Lacruz, 'La brujería en los Pirineos (siglos XIII al XVII) Aproximación a su historia', 336.
87 Ibid.
88 Ibid., 34.

ing sunlight by hanging white clothes out in the sun to dry. Her trial was suspended, and she was freed with only a warning.[89]

The Pyrenean witch hunt had no shortage of witch hunters, some even became rather famous like Joan Malet, Lorenç Calmell, Jordi Aliberc, and Cosme Soler, also known as Tarragó. The profession required skills in recognising bruxes through bodily investigation, searching for the Devil's Mark in the shape of a hen or rabbit foot, on the skin, or the eyes.[90] An ironic prerequisite for many Pyrenean witch hunters was previous experience as a cunning man or renowned folk healer. Tarragó, for instance, took pride in his stature as a *saludador*, a craft perhaps equivalent to that of the Cornish *pellar*, a healer capable of removing illnesses and curses using prayer and the laying on of hands and other techniques.[91] However, the power given to witch hunters swiftly dwindled, and their righteousness was brought under suspicion. In 1617, Tarragó himself was detained by the Bishop of Solsona (Catalonia). His case was eventually dismissed with a warning to retire; he continued to identify and hunt *bruxes* for a further three years.[92] Not quite the same for Laurent Calmell, witch hunter in the area of Roussillon (French Pyrenees). After prosecuting more than 200 people (with 20 condemned to death), Calmell was eventually detained by the Inquisition and condemned to ten years rowing in a galley ship.[93]

In Aragon witch hunters and expellers, sometimes coming from other territories, worked for local law enforcement, going town to town hunting for *bruxes*. Andrés Mascarón, who had worked as a witch hunter and a *saludador* in Valencia, Catalonia and Italy, made his way to Aragon where he was hired by the town council of Bielsa to hunt *bruxes* with a novel procedure of his own inven-

---

89 Ibid., 35.
90 Ibid., 30.
91 Joan Amades, 2002. *Bruixes i Bruixots*. Barcelona: Mèdol: p. 42.
92 Agustí Alcoberro, 'Els Defensors de les Bruixes. La Fi de la Cacera a Catalunya' (2007), 140-156, 140.
93 Ibid., 105.

tion: the 'blowing test'. He gathered all the townspeople and told them to blow air out of their mouths. Those who'd blown out most powerfully were identified as *bruxes*. From this unusual witch finding process, four people were hanged for witchcraft, and one more banished.[94] As fate would have it, Andrés Mascarón was himself eventually tried for witchcraft by the Inquisition of Aragon, although he was never convicted.[95]

The Basque territories had their own famous witch hunter, one Don Pedro, also a *saludador* who'd left Navarra at the time of the Zugarramurdi trials (1610). He not only helped discover *bruxes*, but also helped remove any ill magic from victims. He was eventually reported to the authorities, after which he fled.[96] Despite the fact that most witch hunters were men, there was the exceptional case of a female hunter, Graciana de Ezcároz, who led the search for the Devil's mark among the people of San Martín de Aurtiz (Navarra), finding such marks on two men and ten women.[97]

Perhaps the most notable witch hunter in the Pyrenees was Jean-Jacques Bacqué, who identified 6,200 *bruxes* over a ten-year campaign. He went on to become an instructor in the discipline of witch-hunting. Bacqué, whose expertise was based on having attended a witches' sabbat at six years old, hunted witches in thirty towns across the French region of Béarn between 1660 and 1670. Notorious for accusing up to half of the population in some villages, as in the town of Lahourcade (Aquitaine, French Pyrenees), he was eventually tried and imprisoned in the Parisian fortress of La Bastille.[98]

Unlike other Western countries, the role of the witch-hunter in the Pyrenees survived by merging into other folk magic trades like

94 Ángel Gari Lacruz, 'Brujería en Aragon' (1981), 30.
95 Ibid., 317–354, 341.
96 Ibid., 344.
97 Usunáriz Garayoa, 'La caza de brujas en la Navarra moderna (siglos XVI–XVII)', 306–350, 312.
98 Gari Lacruz, 'La brujería en los Pirineos (siglos XIII al XVII) Aproximación a su historia', 343 and Marliave, Olivier, *Dictionnaire de magie et de sorcellerie dans les Pyrénées,* 93.

the *curandero*, 'medicine man'. Jean Tuquet from the French region of Béarn is a good example, as he originally worked as a witch hunter but eventually formed a group of diviners and exorcists during the 18th century. [99] These *saludadors*, once charged with accusing and hunting bruxes, returned to pursuing vocations in hunting the malefic spirits haunting their neighbours and causing disease. This is a singularity in the Pyrenean witch panic: the witch hunter was not only a symbol of authority, most witch-hunters were also themselves practitioners or connoisseurs of the magical arts.

BRUXES AFTER THE WITCH-CRAZE

BY the late 17th and early 18th century a gradual decrease in the number of Pyrenean witch trials indicated a decline in the witch panic. Those previously deemed responsible for encouraging social hysteria by attacking those who threatened their power now assumed a new, rationalistic approach. This long-forgotten approach had already been iterated in the 10th century *Canon Episcopi*. Fatalistic theories widely accepted by religious and political elites alike in the past were now regarded as naïve and foolish when exposed to the enlightened glare of the scientific method. The emergence of new cities also hastened the decline, as their cosmopolitan inhabitants had no reason to fear the Devil-worshipping supernatural *bruxa*. Eventually it would all evolve into folklore and fiction, and cautionary tales to frighten the children.

In rural communities, the fear of *maleficium* and supernatural entities was endemically linked to the territory, so the arrival of the Enlightenment did nothing to stop belief in *bruxes* or reduce the fear they inspired. The traditional Pyrenean way of living, perceiving and understanding the world was unaffected by this new ontological trend. The vast majority of rural inhabitants had no choice but to cope with capricious, harsh weather and its destructive effects. Rudimentary ideas about the *bruxa* prevailed until the first half of the 20th century in rural environments. People still

99 Marliave, Ibid.

feared the misfortunes they attributed to supernatural causes, to entities which roamed the night. Hence the employment of benefic magic, the use of amulets and charms, and the existence of *curandero* or *saludador*.

In Navarra and the Basque country people continued to speak about *sorginak* throughout the 18th and 19th centuries, and those publicly known to deal in magical crafts or sorcery continued to be visited by the rest of the community. Rafaela Iturriaga, a woman publicly regarded as a witch, received people seeking her consultations about their dead relatives.[100] Angela de Achuri was both admired and criticized for practicing divination and using tarot cards. Seen as feeble-minded and stupid by city-dwellers,[101] these people were no longer considered any threat to religion or God, although as stated by Ángel Gari Lacruz,[102] having a reputation or owning specialty objects like *The Book of Saint Cyprian* could be enough for some to be labelled a witch and an outcast.[103]

Through the 19th and 20th centuries, a branch of folk healers known as *trementinaires* managed to keep the old secrets of folk medicine and mountain herbalism alive. Nomadic experts in herbal remedies from the Catalan Pyrenees travelled the country on foot, selling their products and handcrafted remedies to city folk. Experts in the making of *trementina* (Catalan for turpentine) passed down their knowledge orally to younger family members (usually female: a daughter, niece, or granddaughter). The last documented trip made by *trementinaire* Sofia Montaner i Arnau was carried out in 1984; she was thought to be the last of her kind.[104] These people never considered themselves *bruxes* and rejected that appellation, though surely they would have been

100 Reguera, Iñaki. 'La brujería vasca en la Edad Moderna: aquelarres, hechicería y curanderismo' (2012), 240-283, 280.
101 Carlos Rilova Jericó. 'Las últimas brujas de Europa - Acusaciones de brujería en el País Vasco' (2002), 363-393, 390-392.
102 Gari Lacruz, 'Brujería en Aragon', 42.
103 Ibid.
104 Information found in the Trementinaires museum in Tuixent, visited by the author in 2016.

tried and prosecuted for witchcraft had they performed their crafts during the witch panic. Still, we cannot forget that the distinction between healers and *bruxes* was insisted upon by the community, meaning that *bruxes* were still tarnished with the sinister and nefarious associations of the past.

However, the primordial *bruxa* that flew by night, causing mischief and destruction in league with the spirits of the Dead, refused to disappear. There's an anecdote from the 1940s about a man who lived in Espui (Catalan Pyrenees) who went to the *Guardia Civil*, a law enforcement agency, to report a male neighbour for being a witch and killing his cattle.[105] The accusation, clearly reminiscent of the primordial actions attributed to *bruxes* in the past, was dismissed by the authorities, but the case shows just how little had changed over the centuries: the fear of the *bruxa* had not been completely shaken off.[106] A similar story from Julio Caro Baroja's book *Las Brujas y Su Mundo* took place in the first half of the 20th century. A colleague of the author related that while driving through Guipuzcoa (Basque Country) in 1932, he suddenly saw a black figure in the middle of the road. He sounded the horn in hopes of causing it to move, but the figure refused to budge. As he drew nearer, he recognized the black shape as that of a woman. When he approached and inquired why she hadn't moved, she replied *no ve usted que estoy en el aquelarre?* 'Can't you see that I'm at the *sabbat?*'. Suddenly, the doctor heard some other people approaching and with that, the woman ran towards their voices, into the field.[107]

BRUIXERIA TODAY

*T*HE cases cited and analysed in this chapter all have something in common: they reflect the complexity of the iconic

---

105 Pau Castell, *Se'n parlave... i n'hi havie. Bruixeria al Pirineu i a les terres de Ponent* (2019), 45.
106 Pau Castell. *Un Judici a la Terra dels Bruixots. La Cacera de bruixes a la Vall Fosca 1548–1549* (2011) p. 11.
107 Julio Caro Baroja, *Las brujas y su mundo,* (2006 [1966]), 290.

bruxa. How surprising, then, to find that most historians and researchers have dealt with this entity by applying rather simplistic approximations. The post-Enlightenment theories by Franz Josef Mone and Karl Ernst Jarcke in the 19th century that claimed *bruxes* were people who belonged to an ancient chthonic fertility cult, continue to hold their place amongst contemporary versions of witchcraft. Unfortunately, this persistent oversight displays an utter disdain for the supernatural origin of the *bruxa*. These theories have humanized what must have been a supernatural entity or spirit Double, while dismissing any mention of beliefs in the Underworld or the human capacity for crossing boundaries between worlds. It wouldn't be until 1947 when Arne Runeberg first spoke about the existence of trance-journeying professionals, and set a clear precedent for authors like Carlo Ginzburg, Gábor Klaniczay, Alejandro Campagne, and Claude Lecouteux, according to whom there existed individuals with the ability to control their spirit Double and join retinues of supernatural spirits.

By perceiving the *bruxa* as human and domestic, we lose its essence and the mysteries that were originally associated with it, along with the corpus of folk beliefs from which it emerged. And by considering the *bruxa* nothing more than a human person knowledgeable about plants or a practitioner of folk magic, everything the elites and authorities considered to be witchcraft is perpetuated, having appropriated the same categories and vernaculars.

Witchcraft should be defined as a mystery of the ultimate transgression, the elimination of physical constraints and the assumption of the Other persona. Going with the *bruxes* once meant becoming part of the supernatural retinue of spiritual Doubles who populated the land. Some individuals could rid themselves of the tangible world's physical constraints and become one with the spirits for a while, taking part in the night gathering: the *ajunt de bruxes* or witches' sabbat. The *bruxa* is, was, and will forever be devoid of limitations.

CHAPTER 2

The Pyrenean Devil

I t's time to meet the Pyrenean Devil. Scornful ruler of the Underworld, it grants its acolytes the power to perform *maleficium* in its service, the Master of Witchcraft also easily slipped into roles like those of saintly helpers or bumbling buffoons of folktales. The Devil's complex nature stems from an extensive cultural and spiritual body of influences, overlapping beliefs and visions spanning centuries. These widely diverging roles were seamlessly assimilated, never undermining its integrity. Contradictions lent strength and agility to the moving target of its definition. With one eye on this masterful sleight of hand, we shall explore the masks worn by the Pyrenean Devil and its connections to the *bruxa*[1] in folk belief.

Note that pre-Christian deities such as Dionysus, Hecate, Silvanus, and Pan are referenced here for comparison and should provide the reader with a clearer understanding of the masks of the Devil, without the need to cross the experiential barrier. Despite my initial reluctance to include such pagan or pre-Christian references, they offer clarity when dealing with theological, cosmological, and mythological matters. Their mention is justified by the history of the Pyrenean region and are in line with the work of established experts who claim that the figure of the Christian

---

1 The Devil is located at the centre of the image in the *Tableau de l'inconstance des mauvais anges et demons*, written by Pierre de Lancre in the 17th century and illustrated by Jan Ziarnko.

Devil was ontologically developed through the synthesis of deities and spirits.[2] That said, care should be taken to avoid oversimplification when comparing these different mythologies.

GOAT-HORNED ALLY

𝔄 KERBELTZ, THE 'BLACK BILLY GOAT', is among the oldest masks worn by the Pyrenean Devil. Witches used the name Akerbeltz for the Devil in their sabbatical ceremonies, according to Pierre de Lancre.[3] A deity and major character in Basque cosmology, it has been synonymous with witchcraft and the so-called satanic conspiracy of the Early Modern period.

Current historians and folklorists led by the pioneering Julien Sacaze have traced the origin of Akerbeltz back to the pre-Christian Aquitaine deity 'Aherbelste', whose name may refer to an ancient tutelary deity of goats, one served by the people who worked with these animals, both wild and domestic.[4] Sacaze first identified the Iberian-Basque origin of the name Aherbelste, possibly derived from a combination of the Basque words *aker* 'billy-goat', and *beltz* 'black'. This etymological hypothesis is further supported by archaeological evidence found in the goat-full valley of Arboust, whose name nods to the proliferation of these animals.[5]

The significance given to Aherbelste/Akerbeltz in the ancient Pyrenean pantheon makes clear that goats and similar animals were not demonized at all, but were thought to possess a metaphysical eminence that was accessible to farmers, shepherds and herders.[6]

---

2 For further reference, see Jeffrey Burton Russell, *The Devil, Perceptions of Evil from Antiquity to Primitive Christianity* (1990) and Olivier Marliave, *Pequeño Diccionario de Mitología Vasca y Pirenaica* (1995).

3 J. M. Barandiaran, *Mitología Vasca*, 104-105.

4 This theory, initiated by Sacaze in the late 19th century, has been supported by other authors like José M. de Barandiarán and Olivier de Marliave, whose expertise in Basque and Pyrenean folklore and mythology remains uncontested.

5 Julien Sacaze, *Epigraphie de Luchnon* (1880), 35-38.

6 Mikel Azurmendi, *Nombrar, embrujar*, 240-241.

Evidence of their worship can still be found at surviving votive altars in the French Pyrenean regions of Comminges, Bigorre and the valley of Aure.[7] Assigning spiritual attributes to the goat tallies well with the primitive goat deities regarded as protective allies, like Pan or Silvanus.[8]

The goat is one of the clearest and most frequently cited antecedents to the figure of the Christian Devil. Reasons for this demonization were based on the goat's own natural behaviour: rebellious, excessive, chaotic.[9] As anthropologist Mikel Azurmendi states, "goats have always been an emblem to Basque and Pyrenean shepherds, as their character and disposition stands as a symbol of domestic liminality: the limit between the animal and man, the limit between party and work, and the limit between duty and pleasure".[10] It should therefore come as no surprise to learn that the ruling theological class sought neither to concur nor support the prevailing perspective of animal owners.

We find character and disposition embodied in the 'blackness' of Akerbeltz. Black, conventionally regarded as the colour of death and putrefaction, of chaos and the night,[11] is absorbed in the Pyrenean Devil. When summoned to the sabbat in the Aragon region, the Devil would appear as a black dog[12]—no mere chance, as dogs are psychopomp creatures, depicted as companions to the souls of the Dead and chthonic deities like Hecate.[13]

Black also reveals the bond between death and fertility, as pu-

7   Marliave, *Pequeño Diccionario de Mitología Vasca y Pirenaica*, 157.

8   Azurmendi, *Nombrar, embrujar*, 229-231. Translated by the author.

9   Jeffrey Burton Russell. *The Devil, Perceptions of Evil from Antiquity to Primitive Christianity* (1990) 70-75.

10   Azurmendi, *Nombrar, embrujar*, 233.

11   Burton Russell, *The Devil, Perceptions of Evil from Antiquity to Primitive Christianity*, 66.

12   Ángel Gari Lacruz, 'La posesión demoníaca en el Pirineo aragonés.' (2012) 171.

13   Soler i Amigó, Joan. *Enciclopèdia de la Fantasia Popular Catalana* (1998), 399.

trefaction makes way for the dawn of new life.[14] Death and fertility are intrinsically connected in western, pre-Christian symbolism: in ancient Egypt, Horus and Osiris are linked to black as the colour of fertile soil, the earth nourished by the river Nile.[15] This link persists in medieval alchemy, where black is the colour of dissolution, the stage of *nigredo* in the *magnum opus* of the alchemist, a primal stage of decomposition that serves as a basis for further growth. In Pyrenean folklore, the connection between black and fertility is on display in the harvest festivities held before the onset of winter, a time when Nature and the community must gather their strength until the return of warmer days. In the ritual sacrifice of black billy goats in the Catalan Pyrenees towns of Paüls, Montrós, and Espot, the animal was adorned with garlands and bells and paraded through the town, later to be sacrificed and eaten in a community feast.[16] These rituals, now extinct, usually took place before All Hallows' Eve.

In the Pyrenees, black is given apotropaic virtues and is believed to deter illness and pestilence. An example from the southern Pyrenees is the *Marta*, the black sheep thought to guard against lightning.[17] An accompanying taboo forbade shearing the fur or marking the skin of the *Marta*, as this was thought to disrupt its ability to ward off danger.[18] The association of black goats with apotropaic functions documented in regional folklore survives in rural communities today. It is quite common to find Basque shepherds keeping a black billy goat as a talismanic conduit for deterring the evil eye, or the threat of epidemics, while at the same time sustaining the welfare of cattle.[19] By extension, it is possible that Akerbeltz and the Pyrenean Aherbelste were regarded as protective spirits in

14 Juan-Eduardo Cirlot, *Diccionario de Símbolos* (1992), 377.

15 Burton Russell, *The Devil, Perceptions of Evil from Antiquity to Primitive Christianity*, 78.

16 Ramon Violant i Simorra, *Etnologia Pallaresa* (1981) 70-71.

17 Marliave, *Pequeño Diccionario de Mitología Vasca y Pirenaica*, 105.

18 Ibid.

19 Mikel Azurmendi, 2012. 'A Vueltas Con El Término Akelarre', 53, 240.

ancient rural communities,[20] although it is more likely the 'goat-ish' aspect of the Devil had a greater affinity to primitive Roman deities such as Pan or Silvanus, deities who were revered by shepherds, goat herders, and hunters alike.[21]

Still, we should not forget that the history of the black billy goat as Devil and Master of Witchcraft is intrinsically bound to the Pyrenean mountains: one of the earliest connections between goats and witchcraft was found in the region of Lannemezan (French Pyrenees), home of the expression *Lande du bouc*, 'land of the billy goat', used to refer to the sabbatic plain as early as 1232.[22] Another seminal document, the *Ordinacions de les Valls d'Àneu* of 1424 which was analyzed throughout the previous chapter, mentioned the Boc de Biterna, 'the billy goat of Biterna', as an euphemism for the witches' Devil.[23] These two precedents were crucial to the development of the emerging crime of witchcraft and transformed it into a familiar phenomenon amongst the Pyrenean communities.

TREASURE-HOARDING DRAGON

THE red of blood, of the clay-coloured earth, of the mighty storms and glowing caves marking the gates to its Underworld depths, of the destructive/creative forces of fire[24]: red is another colour long associated with the Devil.[25] Red symbolised

20 Marliave, *Pequeño Diccionario de Mitología Vasca y Pirenaica*, 14.
21 There are evidences of ritual offerings of small weapons and tools to Pan. See María Cruz Cardete del Olmo, 'Entre Pan y el Diablo: el proceso de demonización del dios Pan'. *Dialogues d'Histoire Ancienne*. Besançon: Presses Universitaires de Franche-Comté (2015) 47-72, 54.
22 Pierre de Marca, *Histoire de Bearn, contenant l'origine des rois de Navarre, des Ducs de Gascogne, Marquis de Gothie, Princes de Bearn, Comtes de Carcassonne, de Foix, & de Bigorre* (1640) 826.
23 José Ignacio Padilla Lapuente. *L'esperit d'Àneu. Liibre dels costums i ordinacions de les Valls d'Àneu.* (1999).
24 From the 9th century onwards, both colours would be linked to evil, as stated in Burton Russell (1990), 75 and 237.
25 Burton Russell, *The Devil, Perceptions of Evil from Antiquity to Primitive Christianity*, 60.

the principles of creation and destruction in the Pyrenees before the arrival of Christianity. There are tales of red mythical creatures like the Beigorri, the Basque red cow that guarded the caves.[26] The Red Ass of Bigorre was considered an avatar of the Devil, for it was said this creature could be found standing beside bridges, waiting for wanderers to chase away.[27] The Basque Zezengorri, 'the red bull',[28] or the Aragonese *Craba Roja,* 'the red goat,' also known as Pilou, guarded the treasures in the mountain lands of the Bearn and the Ariège regions.[29] These spirits' redness marked their marginal place and liminal mastery, their ability to move between dimensions unhindered. But there is a numen in Pyrenean mythology which takes redness to an altogether deeper level. The Jauna Gorri, 'red lord', was another mythical Basque creature inhabiting the Anie peak, from where he unleashed the most terrible of storms to guard this fabled mountain, said to be crowned with a magical garden full of plants to cure any malady.[30]

Similar features follow in tales of mythical dragons and serpents.[31] The Pyrenean dragon, like the Jauna Gorri, was described as a chthonic creature dwelling in caves and mountains, a keeper of the Underworld jealously hoarding its treasures. The Pyrenean dragon occasionally displayed celestial features, like the Basque *Sugaar,* the male serpent who crossed the sky in the shape of lightning[32] and gave birth to the Sun and Moon.[33] It should be noted that this celestial orientation was a rare depiction, and the vast majority of surviving accounts associate the dragon with the Underworld.

26 More insight on the topic can be found in Toti Martínez de Lezea, *Leyendas de Euskal Herria* (2004).
27 Marliave, *Pequeño Diccionario de Mitología Vasca y Pirenaica,* 21.
28 Barandiaran, *Mitología Vasca,* 83.
29 Marliave, *Pequeño Diccionario de Mitología Vasca y Pirenaica,* 47.
30 Ibid., 83–84.
31 Burton Russell, *The Devil, Perceptions of Evil from Antiquity to Primitive Christianity,* 245.
32 Marliave, *Pequeño Diccionario de Mitología Vasca y Pirenaica,*160.
33 Ibid., 160.

The Basque Herensuge or Edensuge, another fearsome cave and mountain dweller, is perhaps the clearest example of the chthonic aspects of the Pyrenean dragon, sometimes portrayed with seven heads like Saint Michael's vanquished dragon-devil.[34] Well beyond a mere linear opponent, Herensuge was considered the primeval force of creation and destruction.[35] This mighty Pyrenean dragon embodied the recklessness of nature, the very principle of dissolution, eventually becoming the Devil's most terrifying mask.[36] As Juan-Eduardo Cirlot notes, "the dragon represents the involution of matter, it is the adversary of spirit and the perversion of superior qualities."[37]

In Pyrenean folklore, the dragon was situated in direct opposition to human frailty, embodying a powerful, transgressive, physically driven animality compared with a person's spiritually driven desire to contain. The dragon manifested itself as a natural obstacle to salvation;[38] for this alone the dragon had to be defeated by solar heroes, often saints, compelled to exhibit their spiritual virtue.[39] The terrifying dragon was to be defeated by the knight Vilardell de Sant Celoni with the sword of Saint Martin[40] in the legend of the *Fierra Malvada* or 'Evil Beast' (Catalan Pyrenees); in the legend of the lake in Isaby (Basque Pyrenees), the dragon was killed by a blacksmith.[41] In Comminges (French Pyrenees), it was Saint Bertrand who defeated the beast,[42] and in Ripollès (Catalan Pyr-

34 Barandiaran, *Mitología Vasca* (2001), 80.
35 Marliave, *Trésor de la Mythologie Pyréenne,* 298.
36 Esperanza Aragonés Estella, *La imagen del mal en el románico Navarro* (1996), 64.
37 Juan-Eduardo Cirlot, *Diccionario de Símbolos,* 99.
38 Miguel Ángel Elvira. 'Los orígenes iconográficos del dragón medieval'. *La tradición en la Antigüedad Tardía. Antigüedad y Cristianismo* (1997) 419-434, 421.
39 Cirlot, Juan-Eduardo. 1992. *Diccionario de Símbolos.* Barcelona: Editorial Labor: pp. 175-176.
40 Marliave, Olivier. 1995. *Pequeño Diccionario de Mitología Vasca y Pirenaica*: p. 61.
41 Ibid., 81.
42 Marliave, *Trésor de la Mythologie Pyréenne,* 303.

enees), the local dragon Tarasca was killed by the knight Dulcet who invoked Saint Eudald.[43]

Dragons were renowned keepers of treasure; the one who lived inside the mountain of Canigó hid its riches in the depths of lake Nohèdes.[44] But there were other traditional treasure keepers, including giants like the Gascon *peluts*. In modern folktales, the giant often replaces the Devil, as in the tale of the treasure of the Roc de l'Hers, in Massat (French Pyrenees),[45] or the treasures of Autza, in Navarra.[46] What was this mythic treasure, what did it represent? Some experts interpret these treasures guarded by dragons, giants, or the Devil as symbolic of an unconscious wisdom or initiatory transformation of a person into a hero.[47] If so, these are vestiges of certain deep-seated mysteries encoded in the lands, the keys required to enter the Underworld. Note that chthonic forces, considered as representatives of evil through the primordial chaos seen in the forces of nature,[48] were also integral to safeguarding fertility and rebirth. The treasures guarded in the depths of the land indicate this transformation, and nowhere more so than when dissolving self-imposed limitations. The presence of the Pyrenean Devil was crucial in maintaining the natural balance, defining a complete cosmology and social order through opposition by marking the limits of both the acceptable and the forbidden.

BRIDGE-BUILDING WANDERER

𝕯DLING at crossroads where the Dead appear, roaming the roads by night, lurking in isolated caves and glacial lakes—literary and folkloric sources portray the Pyrenean Devil as a contentedly liminal dweller at physical and supernatural frontiers. This idea

43 Marliave, *Pequeño Diccionario de Mitología Vasca y Pirenaica*, 161.
44 Ibid., 48.
45 Marliave, *Trésor de la Mythologie Pyréenne*, 37.
46 Ibid., 40.
47 Cirlot, *Diccionario de Símbolos*, 261.
48 Burton Russell, *The Devil, Perceptions of Evil from Antiquity to Primitive Christianity*, 62.

of the Devil as an inhabitant of the liminal reflects traditional de-
pictions of pre-Christian deities like Pan, at home in indomitable
places far from urban life, and Hecate, to whom the crossroads
were dedicated, belonging to the wildness beyond village communities.[49] In time, their liminality would link them with other
frontier beings in this and the Other world, whether criminals,
sorcerers, spirits of the Dead, witches, shape-shifters, or faeries.
The use of frontiers connected the ancient world with that of the
Christian reinterpretation of transgressive agency, and under this
more recent guise, the Devil grew into the tempter (from the Latin *tentare*, 'to try out, to test'). Limits and frontiers took on the role
of protecting humanity from eternal damnation, and in turn, the
Devil became yet another expression of the Land, mediating the
way one might interact with their immediate surroundings.

Another read on the Devil's ability to shape the land is found
in the role attributed to Hecate and Pan as incarnating a link for
human beings where nature had become a mode of controlled
opposition. Retaining a semblance of balance for the community
provided a transgressive place for the Devil to dwell, wander, and
rule.[50] This is how the Devil came to be seen as an accomplished
builder of bridges, in Pyrenean folklore. Numerous legends and
folktales recount the Devil offering to help build or finish a bridge
in exchange for a person's soul. True to its role as the naïve fool,
the Devil is perennially tricked by the crowing cock of the rising
dawn, leaving it unable to complete its work, allowing the human
protagonist to retain his soul. Tales like these were used to explain
bridge construction in Saint Lizier (French Pyrenees) and the village of Ceret (Catalan Pyrenees).[51]

The act of building a bridge implied a transgressive act, that
of infringing upon a body of water; as such this bridge-building

49 Claude Lecouteux, *Return of the Dead: Ghosts, Ancestors, and the Trans-
    parent Veil in the Pagan Mind* (2009), 18.
50 Cardete del Olmo, María Cruz. 2008. 'Un caso específico de teolep-
    sia: la panolepsia', 67–85, 71.
51 Marliave, *Trésor de la Mythologie Pyréenne*, 225–27.

aspect of the Devil marked him as a facilitator of contact between worlds. Despite the importance of bridges, their creation and existence was complicated. Some thought that such a feat was only possible through a request for supernatural help. The community might have welcomed the Devil's assistance but once their aim was met they disdained him, forcing its return to the darkness.

Pre-Christian and Christian points of view appear to have successfully coexisted with the Pyrenean notion of liminality and the crossroads. In both views, the symbolic implications of the liminal was embodied by a malicious yet indispensable spirit. Devil-aided constructions like bridges acquired (somewhat ironically) a vengeful reputation as a result of engaging and then shunning him,[52] but without its assistance, the pivotal access afforded in transport and communication would have floundered. The stage was thus set: it was only a matter of time before the Devil, along with other crossroads *numina*, were aligned with the late-medieval witch sect.

SEEKER OF PLEASURES

SAINT Sylvester, a 3rd century Roman Pope, happened to die on the last day of December, memorialised by an annual festival.[53] The 31st of December also happened to be a special night for witches, one of the nights in which they roamed the Land, one of the marked days for the *ajunt*. Evidence exists of pre-Christian celebrations held at the zenith of the winter cycle: in *Cervulus*, a text written by Saint Pacian, 4th century bishop of Barcelona, the bishop complains about animal skin-clad people celebrating orgiastic parties at the year-end rituals.[54] His complaints backfired, mostly sparking animosity and even more passionate celebrations.[55] Saint Sylvester's own role as the patron of witches

---

52 Marliave, *Trésor de la Mythologie Pyréenne*, 227–229.

53 Soler Amigó, *Enciclopèdia de Fantasia Popular Catalana*, 491.

54 Teresa Vinyoles Vidal, 'Metgesses, llevadores, fetilleres, fascinadores...: bruixes a l'edat mitjana' (2007) 12–31, 12.

55 These revelries would eventually be assimilated into the carnival

can be attributed no earlier than the 16th century, when Western society finally accepted and applied the changes instituted by the new Gregorian calendar. But what about the curious attribution of pagan characteristics to Saint Sylvester, a 3rd century Roman Pope? The nexus between Saint Sylvester and witchcraft seems to be the etymological link between the saint's name and that of Silvanus, the Roman god of forests and wilderness, and the year-end orgiastic celebrations quite possibly hearkened back to the Saturnalia rituals held in honour of the Lord of Misrule. Saturnalia festivities involved a societal role reversal, in which pleasure and delight had a prominent role.[56] These qualities would become sins during the early Middle Ages with the forging of the biblical tradition,[57] wherein sin implied the infringement of God's will to behave according to Christian-derived morality. Of all those ancient connections, only a little saying remains in Catalan: *"Per Sant Silvestre, salten les bruixes per la finestra,"* 'In Saint Sylvester, witches jump over the window'.

All deities traditionally linked with what was now seen as immoral behaviour, like Pan or Dionysus, were progressively assimilated with the Devil in an act of homogenisation. Actions that could be called sinful were interpreted as transgressive, and the culprit was seen as upholding a destructive exposition that violated the social and moral ethos. During the Middle Ages, the Devil was generally portrayed with an exaggerated sexuality—a protuberant tongue, lips, and breasts.[58] This systematic accentuation of physicality served to encapsulate the transgressive agency afforded by the church's version of uninhibited fornication. Such contextualised morality meant that any fruit born from unnatural

cycle. See Xavier Theros, "Banyuts per gener" at https://www.ara.cat/suplements/arabcn/Banyuts-gener_0_1501049905.html. Last accessed December 31st 2018.

56 Robert Parker, *On Greek Religion* (2011), 211.

57 Russell, *The Devil, Perceptions of Evil from Antiquity to Primitive Christianity*, 209, 229.

58 Cardete del Olmo, 'Entre Pan y el Diablo: el proceso de demonización del dios Pan', 47-72, 57.

congress would produce further abominations, like the chimera. The church used unfruitful sexuality as proof of evil and sin, and in consequence deities or spirits linked to an exacerbated sexual appetite were subjected to progressive demonization, and so it was with the symbolism attributed to the goat.[59] Intercourse with the Devil as described in sabbatical ceremonies was, unsurprisingly, violent and painful.[60]

BRINGER OF ECSTASIES

A WIDESPREAD epidemic of demonic possession and the presence of evil spirits incarnated by bruxes were 'the primary arguments church authorities put forth to prove the Devil's existence. Belief in demonic possession was already present in the early period of Christianity, so when early medieval theologians claimed the Devil and its acolytes were possessing individuals in order to torment their bodies and souls, it was seen as a rational development of demonic discourse.[61]

The Devil was considered the ultimate agent of possession, although there remained some controversy as to the nature of the spirits commanded by him. Some theologians claimed that possession could be exerted by the souls of the deceased, a belief which survived until the 16th century.[62] Another line of thought, led by Tertullian and Cyprian in the 3rd century, claimed that pagan deities were capable of possession, with the result that exorcisms reaffirmed the power of Christ, first expeller of demons on earth.[63]

---

59 Intercourse with the Devil in the sabbat was typically regarded as painful, as his penis was said to be cold or full of spikes, as stated in Cardete del Olmo (2015), 47–72, 57.

60 María Tausiet, *Ponzoña en los ojos* (2004), 274.

61 Burton Russell, *The Devil, Perceptions of Evil from Antiquity to Primitive Christianity* (1990), 237.

62 Gari Lacruz, La posesión demoníaca en el Pirineo aragonés, 158–200: 162.

63 Norman Cohn, *Los Demonios Familiares de Europa,* 99.

Early accounts link demonic possession to the phenomenon of theolepsy: communing with a deity through an ecstatic trance. Authors on the subject believe theolepsy was socially observed in ancient times as a sign of having been chosen by the divine, although it was uncertain whether the person in question was being blessed or punished.[64] Theoleptics manifested signs of divine communion by suffering from laughing fits, panic attacks, displays of animalistic, bestial, or obscene behaviour.[65] Later, these same symptoms would be interpreted as demonic possession. Unsurprisingly, Pan and Dionysus would be associated with theolepsy.[66] Theolepsy was a terrifying existential state, one that broke the separation between being human and divine, offering victims a temporary opportunity to be liberated. In consequence, being comfortable and carefree were portrayed as a perfect state of freedom.[67] Some accounts describe the deity entering the chosen victim and controlling their will, enabling the possessed to become a god.

Christian communities were in a bind. Understandably, they held demonic possession in disdain, considering it torturous, but to disbelieve in the reality of demonic possession was considered an act of heresy.[68] Possession therefore became a familiar phenomenon, although its treatment underwent deep transformations. The 16th century Council of Trento clearly stated that any custom or belief associated with pagan practise should immediately be excommunicated[69] and as a consequence, the projection of the Devil was bolstered. Growing more tangible and fearsome, its presence was further validated by appearing in texts such as the 1557 tract

---

64 Cardete del Olmo, 'Entre Pan y el Diablo: el proceso de demonización del dios Pan' 47-72, 62-63.

65 Cardete del Olmo, 'Un caso específico de teolepsia: la panolepsia.' 67-85, 67-68.

66 Ibid., 67-85, 67-85.

67 Cardete del Olmo, María Cruz.'Entre Pan y el Diablo: el proceso de demonización del dios Pan'. 47-72, 63.

68 Gari Lacruz, *Brujería e Inquisición en Aragón*, 213.

69 Gari Lacruz, 'La posesión demoníaca en el Pirineo aragonés.' 158-200: 184.

by Peter Canisius entitled *Cathecismus*, along with the famously referential text for Catholic exorcisms published in 1614, the *Rituale Romanum,* to mention just two.[70] The latter served many Pyrenean priests and theologians when expelling demonic plagues, epidemics, and storms.[71] During this time, the first *exconjuradores* or *esconjuraderos* appeared: small, strategically placed constructions where a priest or a conjurer could exorcise storms, evil spirits, and plagues. Notable cases of epidemic possession, like the *endemoniados* 'the bedeviled', and the *mujeres latrantes* or 'barking women' increased during the 16th and 17th centuries.[72] A particularly compelling case took place in Huesca between 1637 and 1643, a period regarded by historian Vicente Risco as a turning point in the history of exorcism in Europe, marking a surge in demonic possession cases throughout the continent.[73]

Epidemics of *endemoniados* affected several towns and villages in the area of Aragon. Provoked by the witch Pedro de Arruebo, a collective possession affected over 1,600 people. Signs of demonic possession ranged from convulsive fits, losing consciousness, to having divinatory powers, xenoglossy, and sacrophobia.[74] The possession epidemic reached an all-time high when the inquisitor Bartolomé Guijarro died while prosecuting the case in 1640, and the authorities subsequently attributed his death to an act of *maleficium*.[75] Only after the accused Pedro de Arruebo and his colleagues were tried and condemned did the phenomenon effectively subside.[76]

70 Gari Lacruz, 'La posesión demoníaca en el Pirineo aragonés,'185.
71 Ibid., 185-186.
72 Gari Lacruz, *'Brujería e Inquisición en Aragón'*, 185.
73 Vicente Risco, *Satanás, historia del Diablo* (1956) 189-190; and in Gari Lacruz, *Brujería e Inquisición en Aragón*, 186.
74 Gari Lacruz, 'La posesión demoníaca en el Pirineo aragonés.'158-200: 174-177.
75 Gari Lacruz, *Brujería e Inquisición en Aragón*, 202.
76 Gari Lacruz, 'La posesión demoníaca en el Pirineo aragonés.' 158-200, 180.

The first case of barking women (*mujeres latrantes*) was attributed to the evildoings of Narbona Darcal, on trial for witchcraft in 1498 in Jaca (Aragonese Pyrenees). She was accused of making people "bark like dogs and other animals, and also while at church the victims would not see the holy wafer when the priest lifted it to their lips but instead saw a black disk".[77] The same phenomenon was witnessed in seven different towns by the apostolic visitor Fra Guillermo Serra, the first person to refer to these women as *mujeres latrantes*, defining them as people who had been victims of malefic magic.[78] This phenomenon continued in 1530,[79] 1575,[80] and in 1596, following the Narbona Darcal case.[81] A similar epidemic of women afflicted by *mal de layra*, 'barking fits', took place in the French town of Amou [82] and in the region of Bearn in the early 17th century. These women were exorcised by a priest with the help of holy relics.[83] In the Catalan Roussillon, these barking fits affected a community of religious women.[84] The last known case of collective possession in the Pyrenees occurred in Aragon in 1812, affecting 32 women although no exorcism was performed, probably as advised by bishop Miguel de Santander, whose innovative approach contrasted with the contemporary *modus Operandi*.[85] Massive cases of group possession all but disappeared after this time, although individual cases from the 18th through the early 20th centuries suggest a latent, long-term survival.[86]

77 Ibid., 158-200, 166.
78 Ibid., 158-200, 164.
79 Genaro Lamarca, *El Valle de Aísa* (1993), 90.
80 Gari Lacruz, Ángel. 2012.'La posesión demoníaca en el Pirineo aragonés.' 158-200, 170.
81 Ibid.
82 François Bordes, *Brujos y Brujas. Procesos de brujería en Gascuña y en el País Vasco* (2006), 57.
83 Marliave, *Dictionnaire de magie et de sorcellerie dans les Pyrénées*, 27.
84 Ibid., 200.
85 Gari Lacruz, La posesión demoníaca en el Pirineo aragonés,' 158-200: 190-192.
86 Ibid., 158-200, 191-192.

Assumption of animalistic behaviour was not always frowned upon, though. There are accounts of an ancient celebration called *Hesta des Gagnolis*, in the Occitan village of Poubeau. Historian Julien Sacaze together with E. Piette discussed this celebration in their text, *La montagne d'Espiaup*, published in 1877, in which the anthropologist investigated a celebration on the night of Mardi Gras. Young people from the village of Poubeau made a pilgrimage to a menhir called Caillou d'Arriba Pardin, a megalithic monument found in a nearby field. Upon arrival at the stone, they lit a fire and celebrated the party by howling like dogs; other accounts claim that they exhibited their genitalia during the celebrations.[87] Sacaze confirms these ceremonies took place until the early 19th century, when a priest ordered the monument destroyed; this was prevented by widespread protests. In 1871, a local priest named Soulè planted an iron cross on the stone to end these pagan practices, urging parishioners to remain at fifty steps distance from the stone.[88] Curiously, the iron cross was struck by lightning, taken by the locals as proof of the stone's power. Needless to say, the event was celebrated.[89] Over time, pilgrimages to the stone were abandoned, and the menhir reduced to a place of Christian worship during springtime festivals.

LAME-FOOTED
SHAPESHIFTER

THE Pyrenean Devil has often been represented as a theriomorph, or shapeshifter. Its stereotypical form was a black billy-goat but numerous sources, from trials against witches and heretics to folktales, depict him in other animal forms. In the

---

87 Marliave, *Pequeño Diccionario de Mitología Vasca y Pirenaica*, 20.
88 Léon Coutil, 'Les monuments mégalithiques des environs de Luchon' (1923), 352–360, 358.
89 Ibid., and Elisabeth Martin, Élisabeth and Magali Fuchs, *Monographie Historique Site Du Bloc Erratique Dit Caillaou D'arriba Pardin*. (2011), 4.

French region of Ariège it appears as a black cat,[90] but it can also manifest as a snake, a dragon, or a black wolf[91] or even as a black donkey in mountain towns of Girona (Catalan Pyrenees),[92] an animal traditionally regarded as a classic psychopomp. Perhaps as a result, Catalan folklore considers the December 31st festival to be the night of the 'donkey mass'.[93]

The Devil shares the power to change shape with its acolytes and followers, taken as proof of their forbidden alliance: this included the werewolf, the heretic, and the witch, all capable of shapeshifting. From the 4th century, authors like Saint Augustine interpreted theriomorphism as an illusion produced by the Devil acting through magicians and sorcerers.[94] But for most people, this shifting ability was far from illusory; people believed it was possible to become an animal and roam the night.

There are ancient references to theriomorphism. The minor deity Lycaeus, after being offered sacrifices of meat, would turn ritual participants into wolves.[95] In his now classic book on werewolves, reverend and scholar Sabine Baring Gould proposed that his principal place of worship was located in Arcadia, home to king Lycaon, the first legendary lycanthrope. It must be noted that this was also home to Pan. According to the author, shape-shifting ceremonies like those described in Greek mythology had to do with the inhabitants' regular contact with wild animals.[96] The author suggests their lifestyle was affected by the many natural challenges faced, resulting in a totemic alliance with potential predators, who were equally admired and feared. As this 'primitive' lifestyle was

90 Marliave, *Trésor de la Mythologie Pyréenne*, 225.
91 Tausiet, *Ponzoña en los ojos*, 273.
92 Marliave, *Trésor de la Mythologie Pyréenne*, 225.
93 El Gremi de l'Art, 2017. 'La Nit de Cap d'Any—La Nochevieja'. Available at: https://gremidelart.wordpress.com/2017/12/27/la-nit-de-cap-dany-la-nochevieja/
94 Claude Lecouteux, *Hadas, Brujas, y Hombres Lobo en la Edad Media: Historia del Doble* (2005), 124.
95 Sabine Baring Gould, *The Book of Werewolves* (2008 [1865]), 6.
96 Ibid., 8.

progressively abandoned, the fear of the wolf shape-shifted as well, consolidating[97] into an avatar of the Devil with its voracious appetite for human flesh.[98]

Despite being admired in antiquity, the Pan-like shapeshifting ability attributed to the Devil, ruler of *were-* beings, became a symptom of the spirit's degradation.[99] *Bruxes*, werewolves and heretics were thought capable of mutating into animals for one of two reasons: they had sold their souls to the Devil, or were victims of possession.[100] These reasons are echoed in Pyrenean folklore: one had either made a pact with the Devil, had (undeservingly) witnessed a magical secret, or was a *bruxa*/werewolf.[101] The ability to change one's shape was regarded as a punishment and aberration (as with possession). This concealed a primordial notion about the Double and the *phantasticum*.[102] Animal metamorphosis entailed, *in stricto sensu,* the liberation of the soul. Pre-Christian worldviews, whether Latin, Germanic, or Celtic, sought no explanations beyond a natural inclination for one's spirit to separate from the body,[103] but Christianity demanded a proper explanation for why God would permit the work of the Devil or its acolytes.

A degradation of the spirit could also manifest through physical disability. Lameness was typical, as in the Castilian *diablo cojuelo,* the 'lame-footed devil'. Some deities share similar features, such as Dionysus missing a sandal on the right foot.[104] Anthropolo-

---

97 Francisco Javier Macias Cárdenas, 'El mito del hombre lobo en la Edad Media' (2013), 29.

98 An example can be found in the 'Sermon on Were-Wolves' written by Johann Geiler in 1508, in Baring Gould, p. 146.

99 Burton Russell, *Lucifer, the Devil in the Middle Ages,* 79.

100 Lecouteux, *Hadas, Brujas, y Hombres Lobo en la Edad Media: Historia del Doble,* 138.

101 Pisón, 'Luzaideko mitologia eta folklore'.

102 Lecouteux, Claude. 2005. *Hadas, Brujas, y Hombres Lobo en la Edad Media: Historia del Doble.* Palma de Mallorca: José J. de Olañeta: p. 125.

103 Ibid., 128.

104 Ginzburg, Carlo. 1991. *Historia Nocturna. Un desciframiento del Aquelarre.* Barcelona: Muchnik Editores: p. 233.

gists suggest that these attributes imply an ability to ride between worlds.[105] This particular depiction of liminality is exemplified by several Basque mythological figures; the *Gisotzo,* the werewolf of Luzaide, the *Basajaun* 'lord of the forest', and the *lamiñak* 'witches', all have either wooden or animal feet.[106]

In Basque folklore, the Devil is sometimes replaced by *Gaueko,* personifying the night and nocturnal fears, appearing in animal forms such as the black wolf, bull, cow, or lion.[107] In some stories, *Gaueko* trap those who dare to venture out of their homes at night, inspiring a famous saying: *eguna egunezkoarentzat; gauezkoarentzat gaua*—'day for those of day and night for those of night.'[108] Christian discourse altered the perception of theriomorphism with the arrival of a more pseudo-scientific approach supported by the Enlightenment. Regardless, this never changed the general consensus on the viability of shape shifting.[109]

DEVOTED ASSISTANT, GRANTER OF BOONS

𝔄 COMMUNITY inclination toward spiritual variance, interpreted as a natural tendency for polytheism, likely spurred the formation of a new discipline: demonology. As mentioned previously, some pre-Christian customs and beliefs held on until the Early Modern age by being bracketed with superstition.[110] Emerging as an enlightened response to a myriad of beliefs, demonology intended to delimit the powers of gods, spirits, and various *numina* subsumed into Satan's hordes. This new discipline became a capi-

105 Tausiet, María. 2004. *Ponzoña en los ojos.* Madrid: Turner: p. 264.
106 Gisotzo is described as having a rounded or wooden foot in some regions. The laminak are often described as having geese feet. Martínez Pisón, 'Luzaideko mitologia eta folklore'.
107 Barandiaran, *Mitología Vasca,* 64.
108 Ibid.
109 Cardete del Olmo, 'Entre Pan y el Diablo: el proceso de demonización del dios Pan' 47-72, 51.
110 Tausiet, *Ponzoña en los ojos,* 258.

tal topic when magic was eventually brought to trial. As a result, surviving vestiges of paganism were re-categorised as idolatry and magic.[111] According to historian Richard Kieckhefer, this view was promoted by early Christian authors like Augustine of Hippo, who claimed that demons could be used as tools to do people's bidding.[112] This claim, according to some, was responsible for a lack of ethnic or territorial cohesion among Christian groups[113] and, as a consequence, those who refused to submit were branded Devil worshippers.

From the 13th century onwards, guided by the work of authors like Albertus Magnus or Guillaume d'Auvergne, European intellectuals began to differentiate between natural and diabolic magic. Natural magic, including astrology, healing, and divination, would later become what we know today as science, while diabolic magic was considered a perversion of religion, and involved denouncing scripture in favour of working with demons.[114] This division was arbitrary and did not necessarily coincide with common folk observations of the phenomenon. Occult powers and inexplicable events were thought to result from superstitious pagan devotion and diabolic magic,[115] and while authorities linked these relatively new demons to evil powers, common folk approached the idea of *daimones* more neutrally, seeing them as having their place between people and deities.[116] Satan actually appears in prayers in some cases: this spell, written by a local priest from Zaragoza, calls upon the power of Satan to consecrate and imbue a valerian root with magical powers:

Yo te consagro, yerba valediana, en el nombre del padre del hijo y del espíritu santo y por satanas, que hagas lo que te pido.[117]

111 Burton Russell, *Lucifer, the Devil in the Middle Ages*, 51.
112 Richard Kieckhefer, *La Magia en la Edad Media* (1992), 19.
113 Ibid., 44.
114 Ibid., 17.
115 Burton Russell, *Lucifer, the Devil in the Middle Ages*, 43.
116 Kieckhefer, *La Magia en la Edad Media*, 47.
117 Tausiet, *Ponzoña en los ojos*, 262.

(I consecrate you, valerian herb, in the name of the Father, the Son, the Holy Ghost, and by Satan, that you do what I ask of you.)

The addition of Satan in this spell could be attributed to the belief that the Devil was equal to God, or at least as diligent when granting people's wishes. Alleged sorcerers and magicians often resorted to requesting assistance from the Devil. This was certainly so in the case of Joan Petit in 1572, accused of being a sorcerer in Barbastro. When asked the reasons behind his alliance with the Devil, he answered: *pues dios no le podía ayudar, que le ayudase el diablo* 'as God would not help me, the Devil would'.[118]

Historian Maria Tausiet suggests the positing of demons was founded on a significant Muslim influence, where they were not considered sinful or contrary to Allah.[119] Perhaps they were no more than remnants of surviving pre-Christian *daimones*, supported by innumerable legends of supernatural entities that help accomplish a tedious task.

In 1609 there was a trial against Pascual Clemente from Embrún, in the Pyrenees of Aragon. Clemente was claimed to have harvested significant amounts of cereal because he possessed five small demons hidden in five henbane pods, familiars given by the Devil for ratifying a pact.[120] Another demon familiar can be found in a 17th century Aragon trial against Jerónimo de Liébana. He promised five men that their wishes would be granted if they made a pact with a demon; once the pact was made, this demon would fulfil their desires. The leader told them that they could keep their demon inside a ring, an idea probably inspired by an ancient grimoire, like that of King Solomon.[121] What is certain from this evidence is that pacts were regarded as an act of sacrilege.

118 Ibid., 270.
119 Ibid., 263.
120 Ibid., 266-267.
121 Ibid., 267-270.

The stereotypical pact emerges from stories about Saint Basil, dating back to the 5th century, and stories about Theophilus, who possibly lived in Anatolia during the 6th century.[122] These two sources became the basis for all topics on the compact; indeed these themes were so prevalent they were still being cited during the witch craze as well as the prosecution of heretical sects, including the Templars, Cathars, and Waldensians. The pact mentioned in these primary sources followed the structure of a standard working contract, very popular in goetic magic, wherein the magician dominated a demon for a specified period of time. As time passed, dealing with the Devil acquired a more fearsome connotation: signing a pact with him indicated the person had lost their humanity and surrendered their soul in exchange for their desire. The idea of losing one's soul, in a time when the soul was valued and praised as one of the few properties worth having, was considered an affront against God.

THE MASTER
OF THE SABBAT

WITCHCRAFT, the art of Otherness, the manipulation of the absolute limit, involves destroying boundaries between worlds and therefore demands a fitting master of ceremonies. The Devil rose as a teacher of transformation, a tempter, helper, and possessor. One of the first manifestations of the Devil as master of *bruxes* is featured in the *Boc de Biterna* 'he-goat of Biterna', introduced in *Ordinacions* text of 1424. This Devil is represented as the black billy goat, a primitive yet familiar appearance: it is the image of a distant past. The Devil situates itself in the darkest reaches of the region, and so presides over night gatherings held at crossroads across the Land. Both *bruxes* and human individuals are expected to bow and show obedience in exchange for learning the secrets it keeps. The *Boc de Biterna* demands worthy acolytes eager to follow

---

122 Burton Russell, *Lucifer, the Devil in the Middle Ages*, 81.

the inglorious path it opens before them; of course, dedication to such tasks demands both body and soul.

Unfortunately, the origins of the *Boc de Biterna* remain uncertain. Some researchers point to Catalonia and Provence as its probable cradle, likely motivated by the Cathar prosecution of the 13th century.[123] Mentioned in a witch-related event during trials in Millau and Lerán (French Pyrenees) in 1444 and 1447, the *Boc de Biterna* was from that point onward found all across the Pyrenean territory. The last obvious reference to him was in the trial against Conilona and Andreva Beltraneta, from Erinyà and Malmercat (Catalan Pyrenees) in 1574.[124] In Basque-speaking territories, the expression *Boc de Biterna* would be substituted by old Akerbeltz, as a more familiar term in the Basque community.

In keeping with the theriomorphic abilities of the Devil, it also appeared in the Pyrenean region in the shape of a man. An account from Pierre de Lancre recounts how ghastly an appearance it could present, although others portrayed it in a more pleasing, even charismatic light. The Devil could often appear as a black man, as cited in the trial against Estebene de Cambrue from Amou (French Pyrenees, 1567).[125] Other manifestations included it wearing long hair, [126] or riding a billy-goat, as Joana la Molinera claimed

---

123 Pau Castell, *Orígens i evolució de la cacera de bruixes a Catalunya* (1992), 77.

124 It would be mentioned again in the trial against Maria Guida 'Tomassa' that took place in Canillo (Andorra, 1473), in the trial against Valentina Guarner, in Pont de Suert, (Catalan Pyrenees, 1484), the trial against Narbona Darcal in Cenarbe (Aragonese Pyrenees, 1498), the one against Granada Sánchez from Ceresa, (Aragón, 1544), the one against the priest Jimeno de Víu, from Broto, (Aragonese Pyrenees, 1548), and in the trial against Margarida de la Plana, and Antonia Balaguera, from Cornudella (Aragón, 1550). Found in Gari Lacruz, 'La brujería en los Pirineos (siglos XIII al XVII) Aproximación a su historia' (2010) 317–354, 331–332.

125 Ghersi, 'Poisons, sorcières et lande de bouc', 103–120.

126 Gari Lacruz, 'La brujería en los Pirineos (siglos XIII al XVII) Aproximación a su historia'. *Cuadernos de Etnología y Etnografía de Navarra* 85. Pamplona: Institución Príncipe de Viana: pp. 317–354, p. 339.

during her trial in 1550.[127] When the Devil appeared as a man, it was elegantly dressed, attractive and mysterious.[128] We can deduce from this that it projected and fulfilled the deepest, darkest desires of the individual. This was not 'a one-way street'. Once it had lured its acolytes into a pact, it sealed their collusion by compelling the individual to submit to its sexual advances. The eventual union of flesh consummated a working contract based on marriage and slavery. As a person's lover it was barren and painful, using sex as a form of domination. It could be delicate and caring, as when it kissed Aragonese Joana Bruxon on the mouth,[129] but it could also be unromantic, as in kissing its buttocks, the *osculum infame*. The Devil demands that its acolytes should behave like demons and evil spirits so that they might roam the night and spread epidemics, misfortune, and pain throughout the land. Its followers were expected to break religious dogma and engage in sinful and reprehensible activities, and in doing so they became accepted members of the community. There were further implications of this pact, including that *bruxes*, heretics, and even victims of demonic possession could only behold the holy communion wafer in black, and as a result they were unable to see the body of Christ.[130]

The Devil is presented as a necessary opposer,[131] a challenging force against everything limited and constrained by both human-made laws. Its existence organises and gives shape to meaning in this world and the other.[132] Through the evolution of the Devil we

---

127 Gari Lacruz, Ángel. 2010. 'La brujería en los Pirineos (siglos XIII al XVII) Aproximación a su historia'. 317–354, 332.

128 Tausiet, *Ponzoña en los ojos*, 273.

129 Ibid.

130 Reguera, 'La brujería vasca en la Edad Moderna: aquelarres, hechicería y curanderismo', 240–283, 260.

131 In some Catalan regions, the Devil is known as *el Fals* 'the deceiver', *el Traïdor* 'the betrayer', *l'Enemic* 'the enemy'. In the Basque country, there is a mythological devil called *Etsai*, 'enemy'. Marliave, *Trésor de la Mythologie Pyréenne*, 220.

132 As in the case of the Basque mythical dragon Sugaar, an avatar of the Devil that punishes sinners and disrespectful individuals. Marliave, *Pequeño Diccionario de Mitología Vasca y Pirenaica*, 160.

may come to understand the development of the concept of evil in the community and according to the church, how folk beliefs and customs have been adapted, and how interaction with nature along with the unknown has shaped human responses. In its image we also find the wishes, fears, and frustrations of a community; here, the Pyrenean community. The late medieval and early modern Pyrenean *bruxa* may not have been the only subject of the Devil—werewolves, heretics, and even the spirits of the dead all shared in this role—but it was the *bruxa* that became the most representative one, embodying the liminal, both human and supernatural, reflection of its master.

CHAPTER 3

LAND OF THE GOAT
Witching Landscapes

ate medieval theologians and witch prosecutors used the crossroad-like geography of the Pyrenees as evidence of its link with witchcraft.[1] For millennia a site of economic and social progress, the association with witchcraft tainted the Pyrenees with the Devil's lurking presence and the threat of *bruxes*. Once witchcraft was established as a crime, the other-than-human inhabitants and the Land in turn adopted a darker, more menacing character.

In this chapter we will follow two of witchcraft's trails through the Land, first in search of the mysterious 'Land of the Goat', the conceptual key to the *ajunt de bruxes,* or the witches' sabbat. Then we will trace the folklore to the actual soil, the physical places which I call 'witching landscapes'. These are sites imbued with belief in *bruxes* and liminal beings, mapped as witches' gathering places. But the less tangible, threshold sites conspicuously referred to as the 'Land of the Goat', including the French *Lande du Bouc*, the Catalan *Biterna*, the Basque *Akelarre*, or the Aragonese *Eras de Tolosa*, are found along our first trail.

Lande du Bouc, Biterna, Eras de Tolosa

IN a broad, subalpine French Pyrenees plain called Lannemezan (literally the 'land in the middle'), we find the first reference to

1 Caro Baroja, *Brujería Vasca*, 149-226.

73

an *ajunt de bruxes,* held in a place called *Lande de Boc*, the 'Land of
the billy goat' in 1232. The place was described as "a land defamed
because it is thought to be the meeting place for sorcerers (*sorciers*)
in Gascony."[2] The Land of the Goat would henceforth appear in
many witch trials; and while scholars and prosecutors relied on its
tangibility and obsessed over its exact coordinates, the physical location of *Lande du Bouc* remained veiled. Two hundred years after
this first mention in French, an accused Catalan woman, Valentina Guarner, claimed to have attended a night-gathering with the
bruxes in the *Lana de Boc,* a literal translation of the French *Landes
du Bouc*.[3] In 1498, the Spanish version of the phrase was first used
in the Aragonese Pyrenees during the trial of Narbona Darcal and
her followers. Narbona stated that she smeared herself with an
ointment while uttering the following invocation: *Sobre harto y sobre espina a* Lanna de Boch *siamos ayna*: 'over bushes and thorns we
go swiftly to the Land of the Goat'.[4] The presence of this enduring
concept grew more visible over time, as it made further appearances in 16th-century witch trials. Estébene de Cambrue claimed
during her trial that the name of the place where witches met was
called *Lanne de Bouc,* a Gascon modification.[5] In a 1548 trial against
alleged sorcerer Jimeno de Víu, the *Lanna del Boc* was mentioned,
although this time it was written down as Alna de Boch.[6] In his
1613 *Tableau*, Pierre de Lancre would be the last to make reference to the Land of the Goat where it was quoted as part of the
flight incantations uttered by *bruxes*: *Pic suber hoeilla/Enta la* Lane
de Bouce/*bien m'arrecoueille,* 'Thorn over leaf/May the Land of the
Goat/hold me fast'.[7]

2 de Marca, Pierre. 1640. *Histoire de Bearn...,* 826.

3 In the Catalan region of Alta Ribagorça. Padilla i Lafuente, 'L'Esperit
   d'Àneu. Esterri d'Àneu: Consell Cultural de les Valls d'Àneu', 53.

4 Tausiet, María. *Brujería y superstición en Aragón en el siglo XVI*, 827.

5 Ghersi, 'Poisons, sorcières et lande de bouc', 103–120, 119.

6 Padilla i Lafuente, 'L'Esperit d'Àneu'. Esterri d'Àneu: Consell Cultural de les Valls d'Àneu, 53.

7 Jean-Pierre Piniès, 'Pet-sus-fuèlha ou le départ des sorcières pour le
   sabbat', 247–266, 248.

The Catalan *Biterna* can be considered another manifestation of the intangible, witchcraft-related location originating with the Land of the Goat nomenclature. *Biterna* made its first written appearances in French and Provencal poems between the 11th and the 13th centuries,[8] along with the mention of the *Boc*, the 'He-goat,' a popular name for the Catalan witches' Devil appearing in the *Ordinacions de les Valls d'Àneu* from 1424:

> ...*Hom o fembra de la dita vall vaga ab les bruxes de nit al boch de Biterna e aquel fara homenatge, prenentlo per senyor...*[9]

(Man or woman from the valley goes with the witches by night to the Goat of *Biterna* and they pay homage to him, taking him as their lord...)

Biterna was cited in trials from the Languedoc area in 1444[10] and again in a 1459 poem by Jaume Roig: *hun boch adoren/totes honoren/la llur caverna/qui's diu* Biterna: 'a goat they worship, they all honour him, in his cavern, called *Biterna.*'[11] *Biterna* appeared in a 1473 Andorran trial, and was identified as synonym to the *Lanna del Boch* in 1498.[12] In 1512, in the trial against Caterina Mora, the accused claimed: *se trobaren en unes montanyes, E lo boc de* Biterna *isqué.ls al camí e abrassàs ab elas,* 'they met in the mountains, and the Boc de Biterna showed them the way and embraced with them.'[13] In 1548, the expression 'going to the *Boc de Biterna,*' would make its final appearance in a trial against Pere l'Hereu from the Cóma de Mont-rós (Vall Fosca, Catalan Pyrenees).[14] Historian Pau Castell

8 Castell, *Orígens i evolució de la cacera de bruixes a Catalunya*, 79.
9 Padilla i Lafuente, J. *L'Esperit d'Àneu. Esterri d'Àneu: Consell Cultural de les Valls d'Àneu*, 51.
10 Castell, *Orígens i evolució de la cacera de bruixes a Catalunya*, 80.
11 Ibid., 81.
12 Padilla i Lafuente, *L'Esperit d'Àneu. Esterri d'Àneu: Consell Cultural de les Valls d'Àneu*, 53.
13 Castell, *Orígens i evolució de la cacera de bruixes a Catalunya*, 64.
14 Castell, 'Bruixeria al Pallars. Materials histórico-etnogràfics' (2018).

claims *Biterna* could perhaps refer to the Italian town of Viterbo[15] or the French town of Beziers (called *Biterrae* in Latin), the latter known as one of the key locations of the Cathar movement during the 12th and 13th centuries.[16] Castell also offers the possibility of *Biterna* referring to a castle in Roussillon (Catalan Pyrenees) ruled by Bernat-Guillem de Clairà, who was condemned for heresy in the 13th century.[17] The term *Biterna* was possibly chosen because of its link with potential centres of heresy.

In Aragon, the Land of the Goat went by the name of *Eras de Tolosa*, 'the fields of Tolosa.' The first mention of the *Eras de Tolosa* dates to 1534, in the trial against Dominica la Coja.[18] In 1544, the location *Era de Tolosa* appeared in an accusation against Granada Sánchez de Ceresa, from Huesca (Aragonese Pyrenees):

> *...ha renegado de dios y prestado homenaje al Boc de Biterna y haun a dado y hido allas heras llamadas de Tolosa y cantando y baylando y dancando y se ha hechado con el dicho Boc de Biterna*[19]

(She has denied god and paid homage to the *Boc de Biterna*, and they have even given and gone to the Heras de Tolosa singing and dancing, and they have laid down with the *Boc de Biterna*.)

DURING the 16th and 17th centuries, there were several waves of French immigrants into Aragon, fleeing accusations of witchcraft. Aragonese historian Ángel Gari Lacruz claims that the origin of the *Eras de Tolosa* can be attributed to a French influence, with *Tolosa* alluding to the French town of Toulouse, popularly known in Aragon as the cradle of witchcraft. [20]

---

15 Castell, *Orígens i evolució de la cacera de bruixes a Catalunya*. 78–79.
16 Ibid.
17 Jordi Ventura, 'El catarismo en Cataluña' (1960), 78–79.
18 Gari Lacruz,'La brujería en los Pirineos (siglos XIII al XVII) Aproximación a su historia'. 317–354, 333.
19 Padilla i Lafuente, *L'Esperit d'Àneu*, 53.
20 Gari Lacruz, 'Los aquelarres en Aragón según los documentos y la

Still, the Land of the Goat is nowhere to be found, as it is located in the Nowhere. Nocturnal gatherings are attended by disembodied spirits; supernatural beings demand that the initiate discard the bloody dimension, and become a part of their retinue. Still, the Land of the Goat cannot be reached in this world.

AKELARRE AND THE FORCE OF PROPAGANDA

𝕴 HAVE chosen to analyze the Basque counterpart of the Land of the Goat, the *Akelarre,* separately from other expressions due to the peculiar development of the term and its relevance in Basque folklore.[21] The original Basque term *Akelarre* is currently used to refer to both the place where the night gathering occurs and the night gathering *per se.*[22] However, this etymological theory has been widely argued, and eventually attributed to a socio-political maneuver orchestrated during the Early Modern witch craze. According to inquisitor Juan del Valle Alvarado, the existence of a native Basque word signifying the *ajunt de bruxes* seemed to confirm an innate tendency by the Basque peoples for witchcraft and heretic beliefs.[23] Historian Gustav Henningsen has claimed that the word *Akelarre* was in fact a false Basque expression coined during the Early Modern witch trials, probably devised by Juan del Valle Alvarado himself.[24] The inquisitor was said to be quite familiar with the Basque language and folklore, so he could have translated the original French *Lande du Bouce* into the Basque *Akelarre* (apparently composed of the Basque words *aker-* 'he goat' and *-larre* 'plain'). This hypothesis is supported by the testimony

---

tradición oral' (1993), 241-261, 251.

21 Nowadays, the word *Akelarre* is widely used in both Basque and Spanish languages.

22 This hypothesis is thoroughly discussed in Azurmendi, *Nombrar, embrujar. Para una historia del sometimiento de la cultura oral en el País Vasco* (1993).

23 Gustav Henningsen, 'El invento de la palabra "aquelarre"' (2012) 64.

24 Ibid., 54-65, 64.

of Antonio Venegas de Figueroa, Bishop of Pamplona who, having completed interrogations in the village of Cinco Villas in 1611,
wrote the following letter:

> *Aunque el mismo licenciado Alvarado visitó las Cinco Villas y otros*
> *lugares con su misma persona, no se entendió en ellas hubiese nin-*
> *guna persona inficionada de esta mala secta. Y con haber muchas*
> *personas ancianas en ellas ninguna sabía qué cosa era ser brujo, ni*
> *cosa que oliese a esta mala arte, ni qué cosa era aquelarre.*[25]

(Although Alvarado himself visited the Cinco Villas and
other places in person, he did not find any people associated
with that sect. Even though there were many old individuals,
none knew what a witch was, nor about things that looked
like the result of such wicked art, nor what the *akelarre* was.)

Thus, the word *akelarre* could be the result of a political and authoritarian maneuver to justify a brutal prosecution in the area.
That is also confirmed by the usage of totally different terms to refer to the *ajunt* prior to the 17th century, as in the 1508 trial against
the heretics of Durango. Prior to the mentions of *akelarre*, the sabbat was referred to as *llamamiento* or *ayuntamiento*, Spanish words
meaning summoning' and 'gathering' respectively.

Other researchers, like Fermín Irigaray and Mikel Azurmendi,
have claimed that the expression can be traced to an actual Basque
lexical construction: *alke-larre*, *alke*, a common prairie grass known
as *Dactilis hispanica*, poisonous to cattle, and *larre*, 'prairie', that is
'prairie of the *alke* flowers'.[26] In this case, 'alkelarre' would not
refer to the *ajunt* but to a location.[27] Following this hypothesis,
the word could have suffered a mutation at the onset of the witch-
hunt, and even though it was primarily used to refer to the location for the Sabbat, in only three months it became the word for

25 Gustav Henningsen, *El abogado de las brujas*, 187.
26 Azurmendi, *Nombrar, embrujar*, 226.
27 Henningsen, 'El invento de la palabra "aquelarre"', 54–65, 59.

the reunion itself.[28]

Nowadays, the word *akelarre* (instead of a more fitting Basque expression, that of *sorgin-batzarre* 'gathering of witches') has been reclaimed in Basque popular culture as a proud vestige of a romanticised past; curiously enough, this seems in line with the design of the inquisitor Valle Alvarado, meriting a moment of reflection.

WITCHING LANDSCAPES
IN THE PYRENEES

𝔘 NLIKE the incorporeal Land of the Goat, there are precise locations linked to the *ajunt de bruxes* and other supernatural reunions found all across the Pyrenean geography: some natural, some human-made, some dating to pre-Christian times, and some dated to the witch craze and its later consequences. Witching landscapes are fully tangible locations that serve as a gate to Otherness, presenting themselves as savage spaces only accessible after the initiate experiences a great deal of personal sacrifice and overcomes the natural, instinctive fear of these wild places. I shall offer a summarised compendium of landmarks associated with witchcraft, and although some locations may be unintentionally omitted, my intention was to include a representative for each region of the Pyrenees.

ℊ *Plains and Prairies*

The plain of Lannemezan (French Pyrenees), cradle of the *Lande de Boc* expression, is among the first locations to be linked to the celebration of *ajunts*, popularly known as the place of choice for *bruxes* and werewolves to hold their celebrations.[29] Lannemezan's abundant megalithic monuments,[30] principally those known as the

---

28 Ibid., 54–65, 59.
29 Marliave, *Dictionnaire de magie et de sorcellerie dans les Pyrénées*, 186.
30 Tchérémissinoff, Yaramila; Bruxelles, Laurent; Lagarrigue, Anne et al. 2008. 'Le tumulus de l'Estaque 2, commune d'Avezac-Prat-

tumuli of *l'Estaque* or *d'Avezac*, were linked by the church to the celebration of heretical activities.[31] Another plain related to *bruxes* is the *Pla de Beret*, 'Plain of Beret', found in the *Val d'Aran* region (Catalan Pyrenees) at an altitude of 1,860 meters, also known as the *Pla de les Bruixes*, or 'Plain of the Witches'. Here is the contemporary testimony of a local inhabitant:

> ...perquè allà dalt diven que el dia de Sant Silvestre, a les dotze de la nit, estaven totes reunides; això sí que és una mentida, hi havie dos metros de neu i no podiven passer, ni que fossin bruixes o cosa semblant. Clar, com que se convertien en gats, també podiven córrer. Diu que se reuniven totes i anaven al Pla de Beret.[32]

> (...because people say that up there, on New Year's Eve, at midnight, they were all together; but that is a lie for sure, as the snow is two meters thick and they would not be able to enter, be they *bruxes* or anything similar. But, sure, as they turned into cats, they could also run. So, people say they got together and went to the Pla de Beret.)

This testimony notes that the deep snow and high altitude prevented access to the plateau during wintertime: such harsh weather conditions demanded that *bruxes* transformed into animals in order to celebrate the ajunt. As with the plain of Lannemezan, the presence of megalithic monuments amplified its reputation as a pagan place.[33]

Lahitte (Hautes-Pyrénées): résultats de fouille préventive.' 187-220, 188.

31 Marliave, *Dictionnaire de magie et de sorcellerie dans les Pyrénées*, 186.

32 Oriol Riart Arnalot, and Jordi Abella Pons, *Se'n parlave.... i n'hi havie. Bruixeria al Pirineu i a les terres de Ponent*, 36.

33 Archeologists have detected, at least, twenty megalithic monuments in that area. Pèir Còts e Casanha, and Jordi Caseny e Durro, 2013. 'Actuacions en Beret ans 2009-2010 (Naut Aran , Val d'Aran)', 164-171.

✚

...Hom o fembra de la dita vall
vaga ab les bruxes de nit al boch de
Biterna e aquel fara homenatge,
prenentlo per senyor...

Among the Bronze Age menhirs and cromlechs that populate this plain, a visitor can still find the subterranean natural source for the rivers Noguera and Garonne. Called the *Uelh dera Garona*, 'the eye of the Garonne', it was commonly regarded as one of the entries to Hell, from which the Devil was said to emerge to conjure storms and celebrate nocturnal orgies.[34] The area, which is nowadays scarred by the installation of a ski resort, still retains its peculiar energy when the crowds are gone. According to folklorist Olivier de Marliave, constant pilgrimages and processions were coming from the nearby sanctuary of Montgarri, a small hermitage where exorcism and healing ceremonies were performed, also used in order to protect travellers and appease the fearful beings that inhabited the area.[35] The presence of mountain plateaus and megaliths establishes a link between the Devil and the *ajunt de bruxes* supported elsewhere, as in another plain filled with a wide array of dolmens, menhirs, and cromlechs found in *Larrun, Larraun,* or *La Rhune*, in the Basque country.[36] The plain of *Larrun* is said to be inhabited by the seven-headed, fiery dragon *Herensuge*, who feeds on local cattle while guarding a precious treasure.[37] This link between the primordial mask of the Devil—the dragon—and the *bruxa* is reaffirmed throughout the territory, connecting their chthonic features.

---

34 Marliave, *Dictionnaire de magie et de sorcellerie dans les Pyrénées,* 242.
35 The area, which is nowadays scarred by the installation of a ski resort, still keeps its peculiar energy when the crowds are gone. According to folklorist Olivier de Marliave, constant pilgrimages and processions were coming from the nearby sanctuary of Montgarri, a small hermitage where exorcism and healing ceremonies were performed, also used in order to protect travellers and appease the fearful beings that inhabited the area. (*Dictionnaire de magie et de sorcellerie dans les Pyrénées,* 243).
36 A complete list of megalithic monuments of Larrun can be accessed at <http://www.euskal-herria.org/megalito/eremu/624>
37 Martínez Pisón, 'Herensuge, Edensuge, Iransuge'.

Mountains

Pyrenean summits have been given names such as 'Witch Mountain' or 'Witches' Hills'. The *Turbón* (Aragon) was believed to be inhabited by the Devil under the name of *Crabón Royo*.[38] Local *bruxes* were said to use these mountains as their headquarters, flying there to conjure storms and leaving their clothes to dry on the hillside (especially on Christmas Eve).[39] In the French region of the Béarn, a 2,500-metre tall mountain called *Pic d'Anie*, shares characteristics with the *Turbón*. The mountain, whose Basque name *Ahuñamendi* means 'the mountain of the goats', was once thought to be inhabited by a blacksmith kidnapped by the Devil, and later thought to be used by *bruxes* to celebrate their feasts.[40]

In Catalonia, the peak of the *Canigó* was regarded as one of the most representative locations for the *ajunts* occurring on Midsummer's Eve.[41] In the early 20th century, the locals planted an iron cross atop the peak to exorcise the evil spirits dwelling within. Each Midsummer's Eve, people still reunite by the cross and light a great bonfire used to light torches, then running downhill spreading the holy flame.[42] Not all mountains successfully converted to Christianity; the *Pedraforca* mountain ('forked stone' in Catalan) did not follow in the footsteps of *Canigó*, remaining instead a forever demonized peak governed by the Devil, the most emblematic of the witch mountains, and the favored spot for witches to meet during the night of Saint Sylvester.[43]

38 Libros del Cuentamiedos. *Brujas en el Pirineo Fantástico* (2006), 75.
39 Ibid., 76.
40 Marliave, *Dictionnaire de magie et de sorcellerie dans les Pyrénées,* 52.
41 Marliave, *Pequeño Diccionario de Mitología Vasca y Pirenaica*, 36.
42 Ibidem.
43 Marliave, *Dictionnaire de magie et de sorcellerie dans les Pyrénées,* 269.

⁊ Caves

Caves and grottos offer solace and a valuable place for hiding, they guard the entrance into the depths of the earth. Perhaps the most famous of all caves related to witchcraft are found in the towns of Zugarramurdi and Sare in the Pyrenees of Navarra. This impressive cave system is bathed by a small stream called *Infernukoerreka*, 'Hell's creek', which became (in)famous during the Logroño trials of the early 17th century.[44] The accused eventually confessed that they met inside the caves, where the Devil appeared as the *Akerbeltz*.[45] In the Basque country, the most legendary of witch caves is the *Supelaur* or *Supelegor* cave, in the mountain Itzine. The *Supelegor* cave is one of the residences of goddess Mari, where *sorginak* are said to appear after assuming the form of vultures. According to a local legend, they asked a shepherd who had placed crosses and protections at the entrance to remove them so that they might enter the cave.[46] The chthonic nature of both the Devil and the *bruxa* is again made manifest in their predilection for caves and subterranean entries.

⁊ Lakes

Lakes are not only the dwelling of water spirits, but also a place of wonder. The lake of *Engolasters* (Andorra), offers a different scenario for the *ajunt*. The first legend of the lake of *Engolasters*, whose name means 'swallowing stars',[47] tells a story of a town that once stood in the place of the current lake, but owing to a local woman's

44 Ibid., 327.
45 The caves are now part of a local Witchcraft museum and can be visited. Marliave, *Dictionnaire de magie et de sorcellerie dans les Pyrénées*, 327-329.
46 Barandiaran, *Brujería y brujas*, 26.
47 As it is the place where shooting stars come to die.

lack of faith in Christ, the town was flooded. In time, local *bruxes* took over the territory and used it to celebrate their *ajunts*.

According to legend, there were two requisites to attend the *ajunt* at *Engolasters*: first, *bruxes* had to ask the Devil to move their hearts to the other side of their chests (i.e. become the Other, the reflection on the mirror), and then they had to anoint themselves with certain ointment that made hair grow on their bodies.[48] Another folktale tells the story of some townsfolk caught red-handed while they were spying on the witches in the lake, and were turned into black cats. From that moment on, legend has it that huge cats still roam the area.[49]

9 Human-made locations

Most human-made locations or sites that provided a scenario for the *ajunt de bruxes* are situated close to primitive streams of chthonic energy, or nurtured by the presence of the Dead. This is proven by the massive amount of *ajunt* locations found near or in megalithic monuments. What once were sacred pre-Christian sites and funerary monuments underwent a profound transformation motivated by fear and disdain. This was turned to the prosecutors advantage during trials, and as time passed and the witchcraft phenomenon evolved, the whole approach to those landscapes was fed by the fear of heresy.

However, the most popular man-made location for the *ajunt de bruxes* is found at the crossroads. The idea of *bruxes* appearing at crossroads will surprise no one; crossroads have long been associated with supernatural beings, Otherworld deities, and spirits of the dead in all the world's mythologies. Bruxes and other members of the infernal host are said to appear to wanderers, especially at night. That would certainly come in handy, not only in devotional practices but also to sorcerers. The relevance of crossroads in the

---

48 Marliave, *Dictionnaire de magie et de sorcellerie dans les Pyrénées,* 159.
49 Àlvar Valls i Oliva, and Roser Carol i Romàn, *Llegendes d'Andorra,* 48-49.

Pyrenees is confirmed by its mention in the *Ordonnances et statuts synodaux du diocèse de Comenge*, written by Hugeau de Labatut,
bishop of Comminges (French Pyrenees) in the first half of the
17th century. In the text, the bishop recommended:

> Excommunicate all those who, before the rising Sun or oth-
> erwise to cure, as they think of fevers, steal from the cem-
> eteries the coffins of the dead, and having broken them, give
> them to drink from the sick with any liquid whatsoever;
> likewise those who encircle the crosses of the crossroads
> with three belts, or cords of different colors for the same
> effect, or who comes with the signs of the cross with chime-
> rical words to heal the animals.
>
> ...that the parish priests of our diocese take care that the
> sick whom they know to be in their parishes who do not beg
> like the poor, but who bring forth nine pieces of bread and
> nine eggs at the crossroads...[50]

For that reason, one can easily find small chapels and iron or stone
crosses in some crossroads of the region, aimed at dispelling the
visit of those entities and granting the wanderers safe passage.

In fact, crossroads are traditionally used in folk magic as the location of choice to perform spells and contact the Devil, as they are
often considered the centre of the world, an *axis mundi* of sorts.[51]
There are many supernatural beings linked with the crossroads in
Pyrenean folklore, like the *Treva* or *Trève,* a nocturnal spirit from
the Aude and Couberes areas (French Pyrenees), whose name
could be related to one of the epithets of goddess Hecate, *Trivia*
'three-way',[52] whose name, by the way, survives in the Pyrenean
town of Tírvia. The relationship between *bruxes,* the Devil, spirits
of the dead, and crossroads is also observed in the enormous num-

50 Hugues de Labatut, *Ordonnances et statuts synodaux du diocèse de Co-
    menge* (1642), 104–107.
51 Marliave, *Dictionnaire de magie et de sorcellerie dans les Pyrénées,* 81.
52 Marliave, *Pequeño Diccionario de Mitología Vasca y Pirenaica,* 166.

ber of shrines and crosses planted in those places to scare potential evil spirits away and offer magical protection to the travelers. Still, there are testimonies of people having witnessed witches' gatherings and celebrations at the crossroads,[53] like the witches from Navata, (Alt Empordà, Catalan Pyrenees), who would go to a three-way crossroads to be initiated into witchcraft.[54]

Bridges, often attributed to the building skills of the Devil, would act a sort of crossroads between water and soil, making them a perfect place for encounters with Otherness. In the Basque country, we find the *Mandabiitta* bridge in Ataun, and the bridge of *Orthez* in the Béarn (French Pyrenees).[55] In both cases, locals claimed to have seen gatherings of *bruxes* and supernatural beings celebrating orgies and feasts at night.[56] Bridges would also act like crossroads in its more practical application, as it was where offerings would be brought. An interesting testimony found in the trial against Cándida Gombal, a *morisca* living in Zaragoza, tells about a spell to marry an absent man: "go one night to the Ebro bridge with three pieces of bread and give them to the first dog she met, without mentioning on the way there or back either Jesus, Mary, or any saint."[57]

Although the witchcraft phenomenon waned in relevance over time, the Land retained an active role as an ally to *bruxes* and their *ajunts*. Most landscapes were more or less tolerated by human population, however, there were numerous instances of locals taking action in an attempt to purify those settings through the construction of churches and hermitages, the placement of crosses, or the installation of talismanic and protective elements. The intense and continued demonization and scorn of the Land has proven to run deep in all the spirits that inhabit it, be they human or not. The wild lands of the Pyrenees will forever be regarded as a deceitful

53 Caro Baroja, *Brujería Vasca*, 174.
54 Cels Gomis, *La Bruixa Catalana* (1987), 45.
55 Marliave, *Dictionnaire de magie et de sorcellerie dans les Pyrénées*, 269.
56 Barandiaran, *Brujería y brujas*, 73.
57 Tausiet, *Ponzoña en los ojos*, 521.

antagonist, a home to the Boc, the billy goat, and a gate to access forgotten lore.

Mountain lands are determining factors to the prevalence of beliefs and customs, specially those which have to do with bad weather. Thus, the proliferation of beliefs linking bruxes and hailstorms will be, as we shall see in the next chapter, a constant association which is even marked in the lexicon.

However, the ultimate reason for linking *bruxes* and mountains may still escape us. British historian Hugh Trevor Roper proposed a peculiar theory in his 1969 *The European Witch-craze of the Sixteenth and Seventeenth Centuries*:

> This prevalence of witchcraft, and of illusions that can be interpreted as witchcraft, in mountainous areas doubtless has a physical explanation. ...The thin air of the mountains breeds hallucinations, and the exaggerated phenomena of nature— the electric storms, the avalanches, the cracking and calving of the mountain ice—easily lead men to believe in demonic activity. ...The superstitions of the mountain are but exaggerations of the superstitions of the plain.[58]

Although the explanation may sound quite far-fetched, it is undeniable that our immediate surroundings determine our perception and beliefs about the environment, and far from understanding the Land as alien, by depending on it we attribute it with agency and volition. Although Trevor-Roper's explanation is now deemed obsolete, current historians have for some time now dealt with the so-called Alpine model when studying the historiography of the witchcraft phenomenon.[59]

---

58 Trevor-Roper, *The European witch craze of the sixteenth and seventeenth centuries: and other essays*, 106–107.

59 More on the Alpine model in: Vincenzo Lavenia, "The Alpine Model of Witchcraft: the Italian Context in the Early Modern Period." In *Communities and Conflicts in the Alps: from the Late Middle Ages to Early Modernity*, 151–164.

Looking back, the history of the Pyrenees, as that of many mountain areas, is one of resistance and of transgression. The mountains shelter the prosecuted, punishes those who are not respectful, and challenge the convictions that populate urban life. In the words of Ferdinand Braudel, mountains are "a world apart from civilizations (...) which constantly had to be taken, conquered and reconquered."[60] it is possible thus that socio-political tensions sparked by the humanization of bruxes in the Early Modern times were not caused, however, by the harshness of the Land and its spirits, but due to religious and political authorities' failure to understand the functioning of mountain beliefs and communities. Detachment from and progressive demonization of the *bruxa* mirrored the detachment from and progressive demonization of human beings from the reality experience in the mountains.

And thus, as we assist to an infantilization of mountain peoples and their beliefs, the belief in the power and presence of the *bruxa* is similarly underestimated and mocked. We are still heirs to the alienation of mountain territories, to the extreme rationalization of the *bruxa*, partly because we are unable to understand the Land as a crucial part of our existence. It is through the Land that we see the worlds as they are.

---

60 Ferdinand Braudel, *The Mediterranean and the Mediterranean World in the Age of Philipp II*, 34-35.

CHAPTER 4

Ajunt de Bruxes

THE PYRENEAN
WITCHES' SABBAT

The Pyrenees is the birthplace of the *ajunt de bruxes*, the witches' sabbat, and attending this *ajunt* or night gathering is crucial to the definition of the Pyrenean *bruxa*. The phenomenon of the sabbat has been neither fully explained nor understood by researchers; as investigations tend to become tangled by the many disciplines and approaches to the topic, preserving a well-guarded mystery all the same. While anthropological or historical positions currently regard the *ajunt* as a complex synthesis of European historical myths and legends, prosecutors of the gathering saw it as the abominable result of heretical practices and a symptom of the decadence of mankind; those who claim to have attended it regard it as deeply transformative experience. The conceptual implications that conform it have evolved over time and adapted in different places, yet some of its underlying ideas remain overlooked. In fact, in this case the parts may be clearer than their sum; the events and premises that helped give shape to the *ajunt's* concept may be visible and intelligible, but it can only be a lived experience if the practitioner resolves to destroy a series of limitations and impositions.

The history of the Pyrenean *ajunt de bruxes*, the primordial night gathering or witches' sabbat, will be closely examined in this chapter, dealing with the nature of its attendants throughout time and history, including the actions that took place in the gathering. We shall delve into the spiritual and symbolic implications within Pyrenean folklore and culture as well as within the broader history of witchcraft, and also review the ways one might access the gathering according to folk beliefs and tradition.

As with the *bruxa* or the Devil, the Pyrenean notion of the nocturnal gathering may be described superficially through an analysis of certain elements found in its historical definitions. However, it would be unwise to attribute all of its baggage to its most infamous historical accounts, such as the prosecution of heretics, for example, or the profanation of the Christian mass in which symbols and idols are mocked as a way to attack the establishment (i.e. understanding the *ajunt de bruxes* as merely a mockery of the Jewish or Christian mass, a conscious attack on the clerical institution, according to a theory outlined by Jules Michelet in his controversial work, *La Sorcière*, published in 1862). Indeed, the choice of nomenclature such as *sabbat* is scarcely helpful to our task of reconstruction: we know that this word was chosen by the same authorities that initiated the prosecution and trial of heretics in the Middle Ages, rooted in the anti-Semitism deeply embedded in certain European communities at the time.[1] The concept of the night assembly as simply an inversion of the Christian mass, or a demonic ritual carried out by heretics, easily obscures the relevant traces of the world views and beliefs wherein the *ajunt* originated. It should be noted, though, that the nocturnal gathering was not always referred to as 'sabbat', but was known by other names, such as ajunt (Catalan), *aplec* (Catalan), *ayuntamiento* (Spanish), *junta* (Spanish, Catalan), *rassemblement* (French), *sorgin-batzarre* (Basque), *vauderie* (French), etc. For this reason, we have chosen the Catalan and Occitan expression *ajunt de bruxes* to replace to the term *sabbat* in this book, as the meaning behind it is less polluted by the anti-heretical crusades, and seems more in line with original Pyrenean folklore. The term *ajunt* comes from the Latin *iŭncta*, 'to bring together'. This uniting of beings—coming from both the tangible and intangible worlds—will prove crucial in the

---

1 Walter Map used the term synagogue to refer to heretic reunions in 1180. Cohn, *Europe's Inner Demons: The Demonization of Christians in Medieval Christendom*, 43.

understanding of a phenomenon that predates the prosecution of any heretical groups, dating far back in time.

BENSOZIA, THE WILD HUNT, AND THE DEAD

ONE of the clearest origins of the *ajunt de bruxes* is to be found in the host of supernatural spirits roaming the nights of the Middle Ages, traditionally believed to be led by a female entity known as *Bensozia* in the French Pyrenees, also known as *Dame Abonde, as it appears in* the late 13th century French poem *Roman de la Rose*.[2] These entities were elevated as leaders of a retinue of disembodied, supernatural beings, whether initially human or not, roaming the Land on specific nights. The first sources to mention them tell of their ability to enter houses through closed doors in order to drink and feast, and bother or even harm the sleeping members of the family, especially little children. By sunrise, order would be restored, and people would usually recover from these disturbing events as if they were nothing but bad dreams; wine in the cellars and food left on plates would appear to be untouched. Nevertheless, the seemingly unmotivated mischief might have had reasons, as described in William of Auvergne's account in *De Universo*, published between 1230 and 1236:

> The same is true of the spirit that under the guise of a woman who, in company of others, visits homes and services at night. (...) They say that these ladies consume food and drink that they find in homes without consuming them entirely, nor even reduce their quantity, especially if the dishes holding food are left uncovered and the containers holding drink are left uncorked when left out for the night. But if they find these containers covered or closed (...) the ladies

---

2 Carlo Ginzburg, *The Night Battles: Witchcraft & Agrarian Cults in the Sixteenth & Seventeenth Centuries* (1983), p. 41.

abandon these houses to woe and ill fortunes without be-
stowing either satiety or abundance upon them.[3]

The spirits that entered houses and drank or ate their fill were, we
can deduce, consuming indirect offerings. In some cases, they can-
nibalised the souls of the living in the intangible world in payment
for granting good fortune and protection. We can perceive in this
custom evident vestiges of animism, a strong interdependence between the inhabitants of the tangible and the intangible worlds, a
fragile balance sustained, more or less graciously, by both human
and other-than-human communities.

The relevance of those beliefs in most rural regions is corrobo-
rated with the existence of rituals and customs meant to satisfy and
appease the army of supernatural entities, as the custom of leaving food and drink or setting the table for the Dead, or even for
the *good* or the *blessed ladies*, a custom spoken about in the 1200s.[4]
Such actions were often carried out during the Christmas cycle,
the Ember Days, and the days near the Epiphany (January 6th).
The still living custom of leaving food for the Three Wise Men
on the eve of the Epiphany in some Catholic countries could be
traced to these rituals.

Considering the Pyrenean sources treating the entourage of
nocturnal spirits, the first written account of their presence is in
a text composed during a diocesan council in Couserans, (Ariège,
French Pyrenees) in 1280. The text, attributed to Bishop Auger
II de Montfaucon, established a clear link between the *ajunts de
bruxes* and the nocturnal procession led by *Bensozia* (according to
Carlo Ginzburg, from *bona socia*, 'the good partner').[5] The beliefs
and customs surrounding the (now called) *good women* or *good ladies* and their retinue of spirits would live on for centuries in the
Pyrenees, as proven in the 1775 testimony of María Ygnacia de

---

3 Claude Lecouteux, *Phantom Armies of the Night*, 14-15.
4 Ibid.
5 Jacqueline Carabia. "Christianisation superficielle dans la région de
   Lannemezan." (2001), 65-77.

Furundarena, who claimed to have seen the *good people* together with the *brujas* and some neighbours while walking to the mill in Martinicorena (Basque Pyrenees).[6]

The entourage of night spirits was an integrating and unavoidable part of Pyrenean beliefs in the supernatural, same with the *bruxes* prior to being granted a human dimension. There was no doubt about its existence, which was taken as a *de facto* truth. But it would not be long until the giving of offerings was supplanted with deterring techniques, such as protecting specific locations across Land like crosses and little shrines, making use of talismans and amulets to scare entities like the *bruxa* away.

The concept of the Wild Hunt inevitably comes to mind, and in the Pyrenean case, it may not be an exaggeration to talk about the retinue of nocturnal spirits as a regional manifestation of that same phenomenon. The spirits which embody Otherness, the night and the Otherworld are bound to reunite cyclically, facilitating the turning of the Life-Death-Rebirth cycle. This could also explain why the traditional date of the *ajunt de bruxes* in the Pyrenees would often correspond with particular moments of the year, such as those around the winter and the summer solstices, as well as any times related to the cycle of harvest or other agrarian events. On those nights, *bruxes*, the members of those phantom retinues and other nightmarish apparitions would roam the countryside and reunite in Lands of the Goat or witching landmarks, standing at the threshold between worlds. In exchange for their part in the eternal keeping of the cycle of life and death, they were often appeased with offerings to ensure their return, but also to avoid a harmful response.

Finally, another link to analyse regarding the origin of the *ajunt de bruxes* is its relationship with the spirits of the Dead, as sources of Pyrenean folklore repeatedly mention the Dead as members of

6 Archivo General de Gipuzkoa-Gipuzkoako Agiritegi Orokora (AGG-GAO) CO CRI año 1775, box 1, process 12, fol. 6 in Rilova, Carlos. 2006. "Indicios para una Historia Nocturna vasca. Brujas, brujos y paganos en el País Vasco." *Zainak*. 28, 449-463: 455.

the nocturnal retinue of spirits. An especially valuable testimony is that of Arnaud Gelis, an *armier*—French term to designate an individual specialised in contacting the spirits of the Dead—who was interrogated by bishop of Pamiers, Jacques Fournier, in 1319. Gelis' deposition in the interrogation sessions is one of the richest testimonies on Pyrenean folklore around contact with supernatural we have. In it, Gelis claimed that the *bonnes dames* or 'good ladies' had been rich and powerful women in life, who after death wandered through mountains and valleys on carts dragged by demons.[7] Gelis also traced an obvious link between the nocturnal processions of supernatural entities and the Dead, proven by the following statement:

> Even if the souls of the dead do not eat, they still drink good wine and warm themselves at the hearth whenever they find a house with a great deal of wood, but the wine does not diminish or grow less because it is the dead who drink it.[8]

As happened with the *bruxes* and the other members of the *ajunt*, the Dead also liked to enter houses and consume food offerings left for them during the autumnal cycle of All Hallow's Eve and the Christmas' festivities. This connection is crucial to understanding the role of the *bruxes* and the Dead as givers of fertility, perpetuators of the natural life cycle. For that reason, in some Pyrenean regions, the Dead are seen as beneficent spirits, serving as helpful household spirits, and serving as familiars to sorcerers or *magi*.

Bruxes, the Dead, and the members of the *ajunt* would also appear in specific times in the life cycle of the human community as well, particularly in those times coinciding with harvests or births. Those apparitions have been explained by authors such as Sabina Magliocco as times of *biological overflowing*, moments in which

---

7 A complete account of the life and testimony of Arnaud Gélis can be found in Ladurie, *Montaillou: The Promised Land of Error (30ᵗʰ Anniversary ed.)*, 2008.

8 Jean-Pierre Piniès. *Figures de la sorcellerie languedocienne*, 241-ff.

life bloomed beyond measure.[9] It is during those times that *bruxes* and other members of the *ajunt* approach the living and prey on them. Such belief finds evidence in the case of midwife Sança de Camins, the first woman tried for witchcraft in Catalonia in 1419. According to her testimony, which we have analysed in the second chapter, Sança protected newborn babies and their mothers from the *bruxes* and the Trip Reial by offering them bread, wine, and a mirror on which they could look themselves. Her testimony proves that *bruxes* were to be expected in such critical times. Similarly, the visit of *bruxes* and their consumption of cellar goods such as wine or grain was also to be expected after the harvest had taken place, as we shall see below.The relevance of the Dead and other other-than-human beings, even though they were considered crucial agents in the perpetual turning of the natural cycle, should not be confused with possible vestiges of a Pre-Christian fertility cult as proposed by authors like Margaret Murray or Arno Runeberg. Murray's theory on a systematic Dianic or Horned god cult in western Europe deliberately ignores the supernatural elements and loose threads found in folklore and trial testimonies. With Murray's contribution, the *bruxa* and witchcraft became palatable and humanised, giving rise to effects we still have not shaken off completely. The role of the human community should not be seen as that of the protagonist in ritual devotion to undetermined pagan gods, but as that of an enhancer or passive attendee—especially in spirit form, due to ecstatic trance or dream—to an other-than-human occurrence. Of course, the evident pagan or pre-Christian substratum of the folk beliefs we have been dealing with is undeniable, but by humanizing the relational dynamics followed by the other-than-human beings that conform this world we run the risk of overseeing other possibilities, ie. that which affirms that

---

9 Sabina Magliocco, "Witchcraft, Healing and Vernacular Magic in Italy." In *Witchcraft continued: Popular magic in modern Europe* (2004) 151-173; 159; also in Fabián Alejandro Campagne, "Witch or Demon? Fairies, Vampires and Nightmares in Early Modern Spain." (2008) 381-410; 392.

not everything is to be made in our image and likeness. Thus, the possibility of human individuals being part of the *ajunt de bruxes* should not be confused with a romanticised and organised pagan resistance.

After all this, it is logical to ask ourselves whether the human implication in witchcraft ends in that of a passive witness to something we cannot fully grasp, or whether there is something else to be done on our part. But let's go back to Regino of Prüm's *Canon episcopi* (10th century):

> It is also not to be omitted that some wicked women, turning back to Satan, seduced by illusions and phantasms of demons, believe and claim that in the hours of night, they ride on certain beasts with Diana, goddess of the pagans, and an innumerable multitude of women; they are called to her service on particular nights, and in the dismal silence of the night, traverse great spaces of earth and obey her commands as mistress. (...) and although it is only her spirits that endures this, the faithless mind thinks that it happens not in the spirit but in the body. (...) [10]

Later complemented by Burchard of Worms' *Corrector*:

> Have you believed what many women who have turned back to Satan believe and affirm to be true, namely, that in the quiet of the night when you go to bed with your husband laying next to you, you are able to go out through the closed doors and traverse vast the spaces of the world with many others who are deceived by a similar error, and that without visible arms can kill people who have been baptised and redeemed by the blood of Christ in order to eat their cooked flesh, and in place of their heart to put something like straw

10 Regino of Prüm, *Synodal Cases and Church Discipline*. Book 2. In Rampton, *European Magic and Witchcraft: A Reader* (Readings in Medieval Civilizations and Cultures) (2018), 155.

or wood, and once they are eaten you can make them live
again for another interval of life. If you have believed this,
you must do penance for 40 days (...)[11]

Indeed, Burchard's text was not written for the *bruxes* nor other
supernatural entities to read it, but for those who believed they
could be part of their retinue, specially during sleep or in a state
close to that of dreaming. And that belief was widespread enough
as to survive through the centuries in many other territories: we
have found instances of human individuals who accompany those
retinues of spirits in the night, in specific moments of the year, like
the case of the Friulian *benandanti*, the Hungarian *táltos*, the Greek
kallikantzaroi, the Croatian *kresnik*, or the Corsican *mazzeri* to name
a few. Those were individuals who could join supernatural beings
in combat-like situations seeking balance between life and death,
perpetuating the turning of the natural cycle. Thanks to those un-
expected survivals, we are reminded that the human individual
can indeed join the night processions of disembodied spirits or
'go with the *bruxes*' in a non-corporeal, other-than-human, state.

Thanks to roles such as those of the *benandanti* or the *mazzeri*
it is made clear that the relationship between common folk and
disembodied spirits that constituted the nocturnal armies of supernatural entities was something to be taken care of, at least until
theologians and enlightened thinkers started writing sermons and
treatises condemning those beliefs and advising against interacting
with spirits in exchange for their favour and good fortune, as that
would be seen as idolatrous superstition, and even more problem-
atic, as a sign of ignorance and stupidity. Curiously enough, that
interaction has served as a way for human communities to participate from nature in an active, extraordinary way. A sort of retribu-
tion for all we have taken away from it. But as we have increasingly
moved away from those possibilities, we have succumbed to the

11 Burchard of Worms. Decretum. Book 19. in Rampton, Martha.
2018. In Rampton, *European Magic and Witchcraft: A Reader* (Readings in Medieval Civilizations and Cultures) (2018), 156.

fear of constant threat found in nature, at the other side of our controlled, domestic sphere.

What follows is a review of the attendees to the *ajunt de bruxes*, those individuals, or rather, the parts of certain individuals who were able to fulfil certain conditions in order to go with the *bruxes* and participate of their actions and their rewards.

MANIFESTATIONS OF
THE SPIRIT-DOUBLE AND
THEIR FEATURES

*T*HE first Spanish trial against a person accused of actively attending the *ajunt de bruxes* happened in 1484, in the town of Pont de Suert (Catalan Pyrenees). The accused, Valentina Guarner, claimed that on certain nights she would anoint herself and fly to the *ajunt* after reciting a special incantation. Then she would arrive at a reunion presided over by the Devil in the shape of the *Boc de Biterna*, the 'he goat of Biterna'.[12] Evidently, this trial set an important precedent in the region, as it had proven the possibility that the *ajunt* could be accessed by human individuals who could temporarily leave their bodies. The spirit Double could then attend the *ajunt* and commit all the actions the Devil asked of them. Delimitating the role of the Double is primordial in understanding its implications; the Double is found in an intangible part of identity, and its existence has been present in a myriad of traditions. Claude Lecouteux, whose work has been extensively devoted to defining the diverse typologies and manifestations of the Double in western culture, argues that the Double is the *alter ego* that can be separated from us momentarily, it can leave the body during ecstatic experiences, during dreams, and it can assume shapes other than its owner's.[13] Traditionally, the spirit Double assumed the

---

12 Gari Lacruz, "Brujería en los Pirineos (siglos XIII al XVII). Aproximación a su historia" 317–354; 331.
13 Lecouteux, *Hadas, brujas y hombres lobo en la Edad Media*, 43.

figures of vampires, faeries, werewolves, or personifications of the nightmare, i.e., *bruxes*.

Another feature of the Double can be found in the taboos surrounding the body or the clothes, especially relevant in Pyrenean witch lore. While the person was travelling to the Otherworld or attending the *ajunt de bruxes*, their physical body could not be touched lest they be prevented from reentering the tangible world.[14] At other times, clothing would be used a representation or *simulacrum* of the physical body.[15] Getting naked would then be seen as a metaphor for abandoning one's flesh prison. This has its representation in a belief that circulated in the town of Tuixent, Alt Urgell (Catalan Pyrenees), where people believed that if a person left the rosary on top of a *bruxa*'s clothes once the witch had left to the *ajunt*, the *bruxa* would never be able to return to its human form.[16]

The shadow—or the lack thereof—was often portrayed as representative of the non-corporeity of an individual.[17] There are many Pyrenean legends and tales in which a bruxa—and sometimes a sorcerer—has no shadow. For instance, Joanes de Bargota, a famous sorcerer tried in the late 16th century, was commonly known as *Juan Sin Sombra*, 'shadowless Juan'. It was said that he had given it to the Devil in exchange for knowledge and power.[18] The shadow could also be seen as the strongest manifestation of the Double. In Catalonia and the Basque country, they said that if one wanted to hurt a *bruxa*, they had to harm their shadow,[19] especially with an iron stick, as *bruxes*, not belonging to this world, could not stand the touch of iron. In Navarrese trials they would conduct the *ordalia del fuego ardiente,* 'the hot iron ordeal', in which a person accused of being a *bruxa* would have to touch a blessed piece of iron, and

---

14 Ibid., 129.

15 Ibid., 134.

16 Gomis, *La bruixa catalana,* 52.

17 Lecouteux, *Hadas, brujas y hombres lobo en la Edad Media,* 162.

18 Caro Baroja, *Brujería vasca,* 16.

19 Gomis, *La bruixa catalana,* 46; Barandiarán, *Brujería y brujas. Testimonios recogidos en el País Vasco,* 49; Amades, *Bruixes i bruixots,* 90.

if prosecutors found a mark on their skin the next day, that person was condemned as a witch.[20]

Something similar happens with Pyrenean *bruxes'* inability to cry or to feel physical pain, as told in Catalan and Aragonese folktales and witch trials, as they are believed to have no remnants of human emotion.[21] This would explain the reason behind the advice of harming the shadow in order to hurt the Double; the inability to feel pain or to cry also contributes to the notion of non-physicality. Also, that assumption would become the reason why inquisitors and judges employed a sharp iron needle in order to find the *punctum diaboli* in trials, a spot in the body that was insensitive to pain.[22] This, as we shall see, would have an important dimension in initiation rites.

The taboo of time restriction should also be taken into account for the Double. We often find references to the Double being scared of sunlight and fleeing before sunrise.[23] The Double is presented as nocturnal in essence; it requires the dark of night to move freely, night being the time of dreams and nightmares. In Pyrenean households, protective devices against *bruxes* and sorcerers were commonly placed at the thresholds to prevent their entrance: leaving a pair of iron scissors open at the ashes of the chimney by night, but especially the widespread presence of the carline thistle (*chardon* in French, *carlina* in Catalan and Spanish, or *eguzkilore* in Euskera), a type of thistle (*Carlina acaulis* and *Carlina acanthifolia*) whose shape is reminiscent of the sun. Each time a *bruxa*, a nightmare, or a sorcerer wanted to enter a house, it would be bound to count each of the thorns on the thistle before entering the house, so the sun would rise again and force the attacker to retreat.[24]

---

20 Segura Urra, "Hechicería y brujería en la Navarra medieval", 303.

21 Tausiet, *Ponzoña en los ojos. Brujería y superstición en Aragón en el siglo xvi*, 334.

22 Caro Baroja, *Las brujas y su mundo*, 223.

23 Barandiarán, *Brujería y brujas. Testimonios recogidos en el País Vasco*, 99.

24 Júlia Carreras,. 'The thorn bush listens to our secrets' (2019).

⁹*Fairies*

It should be no surprise to find that fairies and *bruxes* are indistinguishable from one another in Pyrenean folklore: fairies are often regarded as another manifestation of the Double. This is why we frequently find both *bruxes* and fairies sharing activities in Pyrenean folklore: both can be found washing their clothes—white clothes in particular—by a spring, a lake, or by a river.[25] This connection is also supported by the existence of the word *breish,* used to describe both witches and fairies in the French region of Languedoc.[26] The *breish* lives in caves, has long hair, and is often found washing their clothes.[27] Clothes, as we have seen, are signifiers of the physical body, but more importantly, Pyrenean fairies and *bruxes* are constantly referred to as being found washing their clothes, an image repeated in a multitude of witch trials. In 1471, a witness claimed that Margarida Anglada, accused of witchcraft, had been seen *"the morning of Saint John's day in a meadow with a distaff and tending a tablecloth".*[28] In 1489, during the trial against Beatriu de Conilo (Andorra), witnesses claimed to have seen her doing her laundry during Saint John's Day. In 1576, during a trial taking place in Anocíbar (Navarra), a boy claimed he had seen some *bruxes* going to a river after the *ajunt,* and they washed some clothes in it.[29] Finally, it was said until very recently, that the *bruxes* of Aragon, sometimes called *lavanderas,* 'washing women',[30] would go to the Turbón mountain to hang their clothes in the sun.[31] A

---

25 Barandiarán, *Brujería y brujas. Testimonios recogidos en el País Vasco*, 113.
26 Piniès, *Figures de la sorcellerie languedocienne*, 32.
27 Ibid.
28 Castell, "Wine vat witches suffocate children," 170-195; 188.
29 Florencio Idoate in Castell, ""Wine vat witches suffocate children.";
   'The Mythical Components of the Iberian Witch' 170-195; 188.
30 Campagne, 'Witch or Demon? Fairies, Vampires and Nightmares in Early Modern Spain.' 381-410: 391.
31 Gari Lacruz, 'Los aquelarres en Aragón según los documentos y la tradición oral,' 246.

similar story is told about the Basque sorginak who wash their clothes in the rivers near Oñate, Elduayen, Ataun, and Oxarti.[32]

Many beliefs surrounding the clothes of a *bruxa* or other supernatural entities point to the fact that the clothes are thus to be seen as a metaphor for the tangible body. In fact, the link between clothes and supernatural beings was already mentioned by Pliny the Elder,[33] and has survived in local folklore for centuries. *Bruxes* and other supernatural entities linked with water (like *encantàries* and *dones d'aigua*) are said to be seen washing or tending their clothes on special days. Thus, in Aragón, where *bruxes* are also euphemistically regarded as *lavanderas* or 'washing ladies', and there is a common saying is that which goes: "En el Turbón, las brujas tienden sus ropas al sol", 'In the Turbón mountain, witches tend their clothes in the sun.'[34] Same is believed in the French Pyrenees, where the word *breish* or *breisha* is used indistinctively to refer to primordial witches and to faeric beings who comb their hair and wash their clothes in caves.

According to historian Fabián Alejandro Campagne, the act of washing clothes and hanging them to dry could be interpreted as the power of nurturing and destruction of certain supernatural entities.[35] This could explain why behavioural patterns attributed to fairies are attributed to *bruxes* as well, i.e. the theft of food and drink in houses during the night, or leaving a faeric stock or demon changeling in bed while the attendant is at the *ajunt*, something that has been observed both in witch accounts and fairy tales.[36] Fairies, like *bruxes,* were once manifestations of the Double, whose customary actions, including combing their hair and weaving, categorised them as beings inhabiting the liminal sphere—and dwelling in locations like caves, bodies of water, etc.

---

32 Barandiarán, *Brujería y brujas. Testimonios recogidos en el País Vasco*, 113.

33 Ginzburg, *Ecstasies*, 158.

34 Adell Castán, 'Brujas y seres mágicos de Aragón.' 103-133; 106.

35 Campagne, 'Witch or Demon? Fairies, Vampires and Nightmares in Early Modern Spain.' 381-410; 391.

36 Wilby, *Cunning Folk and Familiar Spirits*, 178.

which are connected to the source of power found throughout the Land. Nonetheless, while fairies have often been attributed to a literary creation from the Middle Ages,[37] *bruxes* prove to be an endemic presence in mountain folklore. Fairies could have originated as members of the night host, but were later transformed into friendlier characters, helpers, influenced by the ideals born during the romantic era or the aesthetics of *art nouveau*, a process never undergone by the *bruxa*.

ꝯ *Shapeshifters and Werewolves*

Another manifestation of the Double is that of the werewolf, or more generally, a theriomorph or shape-shifter, that is a person who can transform into an animal. Pyrenean folklore again makes no distinction between witches and shapeshifters. In fact, judge Pierre de Lancre compares the followers of Diana to werewolves.[38] An idea that comes from Roman antiquity when werewolves, like witches, were believed to transform into animals for a determined period of time, such as seven or nine-year periods.[39] Werewolves in other countries, especially in northern European regions, are often portrayed as entering cellars and emptying barrels of wine, an action traditionally attributed to *strigae* or the primordial *bruxes* which shall be dealt with below.[40] We also find tales and legends in which *bruxes* are transformed into animals: a wolf, cat, fox, pig, donkey, horse,[41] lamb, sheep, ram, cow,[42] or even a fly or an ant.[43] In contrast, werewolves, known as *loups-garous* in the French Pyrenees, are usually portrayed as exclusively transforming into wolves, or dogs. However, it is important to state that, according

37 Campagne, 'Witch or Demon? Fairies, Vampires and Nightmares in Early Modern Spain', 381–410: 390.

38 Ginzburg, *Ecstasies*, 137.

39 Ibid., 158.

40 Ibid.

41 Barandiarán, *Brujería y brujas. Testimonios recogidos en el País Vasco*, 41.

42 Piniès, *Figures de la sorcellerie languedocienne*, 85.

43 Barandiarán, *Brujería y brujas. Testimonios recogidos en el País Vasco*, 46.

to Pyrenean folklore, the gender of the human individual often dictated the animal in which he or she would turn into. Thus, men would often turn into wolves and women into cats, but there are examples that seem to connect wolves with women as well. In the region of Lannemezan, people said that female *bruxes* could also be *loup-garous* as they had all been punished by the Devil.[44]

Another proof of the interrelation between werewolves and *bruxes* is again found in the clothing taboo as presented in a 12th century folk tale from France, in which a woman who wishes to get rid of her werewolf husband takes his clothes, so he cannot return to human form.[45] The werewolf's clothes, mentioned for the first time by Roman historian Pliny,[46] are as the *bruxa's*, a representation of the human form, the physical body, temporarily abandoned. In Bigorre (French Pyrenees), *loups-garous* are believed capable of attending the *ajunt de bruxes* thanks to a pact with Satan.[47] Again, if one wishes to harm them they only have to harm their shadow.[48] Finally, there is a Basque belief according to which some sorcerers can turn into werewolves when washing themselves in a specific fountain on Saint John's Eve.[49]

When shapeshifting, the Double disguises as an animal to abandon the body, either to commit special acts or to traverse otherwise impossible distances. In a sermon found in the inquisitorial register of Jacques Fournier (14th century), we are told the story of a christian (heretic, in this case), whose soul was considered able to abandon the body in the shape of a little lizard while the person was asleep: it would crawl from his mouth, enter a larger animal's mouth and take control of the animal recipient, cross a

---

44 Dubourg, *Histoire des sorcières et sorciers dans le Sud-Ouest*, 43.
45 Marie De France, *Le livre de poche*, 120-121. In Javier Macias Cárdenas, "El mito del hombre lobo en la Edad Media" (2013) 28-37.
46 Ginzburg, *Ecstasies*, 158.
47 Roques, *Sorcellerie et superstitions dans les Pyrénées centrales du XVIe au XIXe siècle*, 100.
48 Ibid., 101.
49 Dubourg, *Histoire des sorcières et sorciers dans le Sud-Ouest*, 43.

stream, and would finally return to the sleeper again through the mouth cavity.[50]

Bruxes would use their shapeshifting abilities and become animals in order to fly or travel swiftly to the *ajunt*. Other common beliefs claimed that *bruxes* could turn into hares,[51] or in the case of the Basque *lamiñak*, which would turn into vultures when they were next to the cave of Superlaun.[52] This would be proven by the numerous mentions of shapeshifting in Pyrenean witch trials, as the case of Ana Pomadera, accused of turning into a cat or a dog, in the Pyrenees of Aragon.[53] Also the case of María Persona, from the Basque Pyrenees, who would claim that she and her colleagues would transform into animals when going to the *ajunt*.[54] As Graciana de Barrenechea, known as the queen of the ajunt in the Zugarramurdi (Navarra), whom the Devil had transformed into a mare.[55]

Esteban de Borbón, 13th century inquisitor, claimed that *bruxes* could enter through closed doors either riding a wolf or assuming its shape. If somebody had the chance to mark the animal with a red iron, they would be able to find the human the next morning.[56] The story would be repeated innumerable times in the Pyrenean folk tales from the late Middle Ages to the 20th century: proof of this can be found in a 1920s Durango folktale in which a local woman found a cat bothering her child. The woman kicked the cat out of the house with a broom, and the next day she found that an

50 Duvernoy, *Le Registre d'Inquisition Jacques Fournier (Evêque de Pamiers)*, 945.
51 Caro Baroja, *Brujería vasca*, 135.
52 Barandiarán, *Brujería y brujas. Testimonios recogidos en el País Vasco*, 28.
53 Gari Lacruz, 'Los aquelarres en Aragón según los documentos y la tradición oral.' 241-261; 256.
54 Caro Baroja, *Las brujas y su mundo*, 231.
55 Manuel Fernandez Nieto. *Proceso a la brujería. En torno al auto de fe de los brujos de ugarramurdi, Logroño, 1610.* (1989) 45.
56 Lecouteux, *Hadas, brujas y hombres lobo en la Edad Media*, 95.

old local woman had been struck in the same spot as the cat.[57] The same story that can also be found in Catalonia,[58] and in Aragon.[59]

HUMANS WHO GO WITH THE *BRUXES*

𝕿HE belief in the human Double was actively prosecuted in Pamiers (French Pyrenees), when Jacques Fournier argued that it was proof of heresy to claim that there were two rational substances in man, i.e., that there were two spirits, or a soul and a spirit (understood as *daimon*), and that one of them could leave the body.[60] However, there were human beings who could (or believed they could) follow the retinue of supernatural beings by separating one of the parts of their spirit from their bodies. Those individuals able to free the double at will may have been regarded as *professional ecstatics*, as suggested by Claude Lecouteux,[61] but often were instead described as heretics or possessed.[62] In order to follow the spectral retinues and the *bruxes*, the individual had to be able to separate their Double from the body temporarily—or as Pierre de Lancre claimed in the 17th century, at least have a certain ability to fall in diabolical ecstasy and to succumb to the wishes of Devil was at least required.[63]

But how was the experience of detaching the spirit Double from the body and joining the gathering regarded in the past? For Martin d'Arles, 14th century bishop of Avila, the *ajunt de bruxes* happened in dreams;[64] however, that does not mean that he considered it unreal. Dreams were thought to be another manifestation of reality. To Anne-Marie Georgel and Caterine Delort, two women

57 Barandiarán, *Brujería y brujas. Testimonios recogidos en el País Vasco*, 32.

58 Gomis, *La bruixa catalana*, 49.

59 Tausiet, *Ponzoña en los ojos*, 359.

60 Duvernoy, *Le Registre d'Inquisition Jacques Fournier (Evêque de Pamiers)*, 999.

61 Lecouteux, *Hadas, brujas y hombres lobo en la Edad Media*, 47.

62 Ibid.,73.

63 Ginzburg, *Ecstasies*, 137.

64 Lecouteux, *Hadas, brujas y hombres lobo en la Edad Media*, 10.

accused of witchcraft in Toulouse in 1335, the *ajunt* was effectively accessed by night in an *extraordinary dream*.[65] Even though their tangible bodies did not move, their Doubles attended the *ajunt*, and that was taken as truth. Such an approach would explain why the most recognisable abilities of the Double would be passing through closed doors or small holes in the wall.[66] It seems that the necessary feature for becoming part of the *ajunt de bruxes* was the transgression of the tangible dimension, a transitory elimination of the physical self, *via temporary death*.[67]

Ecstatic journeys and its vehicles (which we will deal with in detail below) allowed the human being to catch a glimpse of the otherworld, and to return after going with the *bruxes* with perhaps valuable knowledge. To many readers, such occurrences had a lot to do with the traditional concept of shamanism, as the Spirit Flight to the *ajunt* can be seen as another take on the shamanic journey. However, there is some difference between the theory of the spirit Double and shamanism. We should remember that shamanism is traditionally regarded as part of a cultural complex born in Siberian communities and an integrative part of community living, ie. the shaman is publicly recognised as such by his fellow peers. But when dealing with *bruxes* and other manifestations of the Double, it seems the experience was mainly individual and private.[68]

Of course, there were some exceptions to that rule. There were individuals whose tasks involved some degree of ecstatic journey or interaction with the spirit world, and whose resulting experiences were share with and used by the community. Perhaps the most paradigmatic case in the Pyrenees is that of Arnaud Gélis, which has been brought up before, an Occitan *armier* or *armarié* questioned by Jacques Fournier in 1319. Gelis claimed to be able to see the souls of dead people, and speak with them. Gelis also

---

65 Ibid., 104.
66 Barandiarán, *Brujería y brujas. Testimonios recogidos en el País Vasco*, 81.
67 Ginzburg, *Ecstasies*, 100.
68 Campagne, 'Witch or Demon? Fairies, Vampires and Nightmares in Early Modern Spain', 381-410: 395.

maintained he had the obligation to communicate the messages he received from dead people, or he would suffer terrible punishments. His experiences happened both at night while in bed, and during the day while at work. His interrogation revealed important pieces of information and petitions coming from the realm of the dead. Here is a quite interesting fragment containing some of his observations:

> The dead felt the cold, and at night they would go to houses with a good supply of logs and light a fire in the hearth from the embers which the living had covered up before going to bed (i.128,139, 537, 545, 548). The dead did not eat, but they did drink wine, and very good wine at that. At night they would go and empty the barrels in the finest and cleanest houses. (According to another version, the level of wine in the barrel did not go down.) Before the harvest, Gelis joined in veritable drinking bouts with the dead, in parties of over a hundred. He drank his share - it may have been this which earned him the nickname 'Bottler' (...) But there was no question of the dead enjoying the pleasures of the flesh, or of family life in the full meaning of the term. They had no houses of their own, though they frequently visited the houses they used to live in as well as the homes of others. [69]

Again, his claim seems in line with the belief in the systematic entering into houses and consumption of liquids attributed to *bruxes* and werewolves.From his observations it was also deduced that the dead wanted to be visited often by the living; they liked having masses said in their honour, and liked to undo all the harm and injustices they had committed in life.[70] In most cases, the dead told Gelis not to fear eternal damnation, as there was no hell or heaven, and the souls of the dead inhabited purgatory until Judgement Day. Gelis also said that the dead enjoyed going from church

---

69 Ladurie, *Montaillou: The Promised Land of Error*, 347-8.
70 For a full account on Gelis's testimony see Ladurie, *Montaillou*.

to church along old roads; once their penance was complete, they returned to the earth to wait until Judgement Day. Nevertheless, Arnaud Gelis had to retract all his affirmations in the end, else he would have been tried for heresy by the Inquisition.

Gelis's role as well as that of the armiers was that of a companion to the spirits, one who participated of their periodical visits and consort with them. But Gelis's awareness and daily participation was not the rule, since most individuals would experience such events in an uncontrolled and spontaneous fashion.

GOING WITH THE *BRUXES*

As the reader may have deduced, there is no detailed methodology to go with the bruxes, but one can only decode that glyph by putting the bits of folklore together and read between the lines, separating religious and authoritarian propaganda from actual events or beliefs supported by the community. What follows is a series of beliefs attributed to *bruxes* and what happens during the *ajunt*, which may or may not be taken as mysteric keys for the initiated.

¶ *Emptying cellars, crushing chests, and sucking blood*

Nocturnal spirits that formed the night assembly were given offerings in exchange for prosperity, but also reportedly committed mischief, emptying wine from cellars, disturbing sleepers, or even abducting, harming, and killing cattle or people. Those actions were discussed as early as the 10th century by Regino of Prüm and in 1212 by Gervais of Tilbury in his *Otia Imperialia*, disserting about those who went with the *lamiae*.[71] It was thought that denying those spirits what they came for would cause a terrible reaction. Such beliefs would persist throughout the Middle Ages, becoming a common accusation against flesh and blood individuals in several

---

71 Gervasius Von Tilbury, Otia imperialia. *De phantasiis, nocturnis opiniones XCIII*, 992 (45).

witch trials, e.g., in the 1575 Navarrese trial against Maria Johan, said to be able to enter closed windows and doors. The same occurred in the Aragonese trials of 1657, when the accused were said to fly through tiny holes in doors to attend the *ajunt* at Bordeaux.[72] Those beliefs were maintained along the Pyrenees until the 1970s, as shown by research conducted by French ethnologist Jean-Pierre Piniès, who verified the survival of the folk belief in *La Fumée*, a male being described as a nightmarish being able to enter through closed doors and windows.[73]

The link between *bruxes* and the systematic emptying of wine casks and harming people by night can also be observed in a trial that took place in 1471 in the region of Urgell (Catalan Pyrenees), where the accused Guillema Casala declared herself guilty of breaking into houses at night, drinking wine and dancing, before *bruxar* ('crushing') a child,[74] a story that would be repeated in 1548 in the territory of Mont-rós (Catalan Pyrenees), in which an accused confessed that:

> They entered the house and went to the chamber, where they crushed a little child. ...Having crushed the little child, they took bread and they went to the cellar and took wine out of a vat. ...And they also spilled the grain from a chest.[75]

This action would finally be given an explanation at an Aragonese trial in 1571, in which a conversation about witches and wine between a young witness and her mother was transcribed:

> *Madre, agora no hay broxas [...] Hija, agora no es tiempo de andar, que hay poco vino, que quando hay mucho vino las broxas de las*

---

72 Campagne, 'Witch or Demon? Fairies, Vampires and Nightmares in Early Modern Spain' 381–410; 384–385.

73 Piniès, *Figures de la sorcellerie languedocienne*, 94–95.

74 Castell,"'Wine vat witches suffocate children," 170–195; 189.

75 Ibid., 189. Translated from Catalan by Pau Castell.

cubas ahogan las criaturas.[76]

(Mother, there are no witches now [...] Daughter, now it is not time to walk, as there is little wine, but when there is much wine the wine vat witches suffocate children.)

In this conversation, the mother tells her daughter that there was no danger of being attacked by *bruxes* since there was little wine, showing a clear correlation between the time of the harvest or *biological overflowing*, supernatural wine consumption, and infanticide.

Unsurprisingly, a similar accusation was made against the Friulian benandante Paolo Gasparutto, tried in 1575. In his testimony, Gasparutto gave a quite revealing testimony on the malandanti, against whom the benandanti fought in spirit battles:

...the men and women who are the *malandanti* carry and use the sorghum stalks which grow in the fields, and the men and women who are benandanti use fennel stalks; and they go now one day and now another, but always on Thursdays, and...when they make their great displays they go to the biggest farms, and they have days fixed for this; and when the warlocks and witches set out it is to do evil, and they must be pursued by the benandanti to thwart them, and also to stop them from entering the houses, because if they do not find clear water in the pails they go into the cellars and spoil the wine with certain things, throwing filth in the bungholes.

Bruxes and other supernatural spirits embodying otherness like the spirits of the Dead certainly have certainly a predilection for visiting the houses of sleepers and punish those who acknowledge them with offerings by spoiling their wine or the fruits of their harvest.

Also, *bruxes*, and by extension, those accused of going with

---

76 Tausiet, 'Brujería y metáfora: el infanticidio y sus traducciones en Aragón, s. XVI-XVII' 61-83: 76-77.

them, were feared for their inclination to attack sleepers. In a testimony told by Magdalena Ricarda in 1471 (Catalan Pyrenees), who claimed that she had been attacked and scratched by a *bruxa* the night after giving birth.[77] There is also the testimony given by Joan de Riu, who claimed his wife was attacked by a *bruxa* that grabbed her breast, and that her wife had to be revived with fumigations.[78] Or in Seix (Ariège, French Pyrenees) where in 1562 a collective of *poisonières* ('poison-makers') were tried for suffocating children by pressing their chests.[79] As stated in Basque witch trials, *sorginak* are able to *chupar el seso* 'suck the marrow' of people.[80] Catalina de Somiano was accused of being caught biting and sucking the blood of several women, whose bodies displayed bruises or needle marks. The victims also showed signs of extreme exhaustion after those phenomena.[81] In some cases, the death of children or cattle would also be interpreted as failed attempts to attack an adult, as seen in the trial against Beatriu de Conilo (1489) in Andorra. A mare was found dead in the barn and the neighbour said: "God has shown you mercy. They haven't got power over you or your wife, and then it has happened to the mare, since it was you or your wife that *bruxes* were to kill".[82]

In this sense, those testimonies also seem in line with the widespread presence of nightmare-like creatures in Pyrenean folklore, such as the Basque *inguma*,[83] the Occitan *sarramauca*,[84] or the Catalan *pesanta*,[85] all famous for their crushing the sleepers' chests, and

77 Castell, 'Wine vat witches suffocate children: The Mythical Components of the Iberian Witch.' 170-195; 185-186.

78 Ibid.

79 Campagne, 'Witch or Demon? Fairies, Vampires and Nightmares in Early Modern Spain.' 381-410; 402.

80 Caro Baroja, *Brujería vasca*, 114.

81 Reguera, 'La brujería vasca en la Edad Moderna: aquelarres, hechicería y curanderismo,' 267.

82 Castell, '"Wine vat witches suffocate children." The Mythical Components of the Iberian Witch.' 170-195; p. 186.

83 Marliave, *Pequeño Diccionario de Mitología Vasca y Pirenaica*, 80.

84 Ibid., 53.

85 Ibid., 133.

suffocating them. Those beings were often considered equivalent to *bruxes*, who in turn were often considered manifestations of the nightmare.[86] An example of such ambivalence worth mentioning can be found in Huesca, Aragon, in the trial against Águeda Ruiz in 1591:

> *Habrá dos años poco mas o menos, estando esta deposante recién parida, una noche, y teniendo en el aposento una lampara encendida junto a la cama donde dormía, y estando despierta, entre once y doce oras de dicha noche poco mas o menos, vio esta deposante a los dos lados de dicha cama dos mugeres. Y esta deposante, como las vio, se espanto toda. Y como tenia la dicha lampara encendida, vio y conocio muy bien a las dichas dos mugeres, las cuales se llamaban Agueda Ruyz (...) y Joana de Liesa (...) procuro quanto pudo esconderse y despertar al dicho su marido, y no pudo jamas, por mucho que hizo.*

(Two years ago, more or less, right after the witness had given birth, one night, and having a light by the bed where she slept, between eleven and twelve at night, she witnessed two different women, one at each side of the bed. And the witness, as she saw them, was terrified. And as the light was on, she could see them and recognize them clearly, who were Agueda Ruyz and Joana de Liesa...she tried to hide and wake her husband, but she couldn't, as hard as she tried.)[87]

The actions attributed to the nightmare would often be parallel those attributed to the *bruxa*: the attack and cannibalising of infants, human, and cattle, and the engagement in vampiric activity, which served as a prelude or, less frequently, conclusion to the nocturnal assemblies. However, perhaps because of the primordial

---

86 Campagne, 'Witch or Demon? Fairies, Vampires and Nightmares in Early Modern Spain.' 381-410: 394.

87 AHPH C 1211-8, fol 81 in Tausiet, *Ponzoña en los ojos. Brujería y superstición en Aragón en el siglo xvi.*, p. 350.

aspect of the *bruxa*, those activities seem more prominent in the Pyrenees than in other territories,[88] as the accusation of cannibalism and vampirism would repeatedly appear in witch trials in the area. Such an anecdote was related by Ricarda Berenguer in 1471, when a she saw someone from her village climbing into her babies' cradle and attempting to take away her new-born children,[89] or in a 1561 trial in the Basque town of Sopuerta, in which the accused confessed to killing children.[90] Or in 1572, when Mayora de Cenáuri was accused of sucking the blood of little children *por la natura* ('through their genitalia') before they were baptised.[91] The protection of children was a paramount issue, as attested by the existence of the famous *ristras* or *rastras de bautizo*, a special type of belt sewn into unbaptized babies' clothes and filled with amulets and protective talismans: badger claws, red coral horns, etc.[92] In most cases, both *bruxes* and nightmares could only be expelled by making them count things, by uttering of prayer and invocation of the Virgin Mary, or with the light of the sun.[93] However, as we have argued, the possibility existed for a human individual to become one of the nightmare creatures, and conditions would establish a link with other manifestations of the Double: if born the consecutive seventh or fifth daughter, a woman could become one of the nightmares, but if it were a man born after four or six consecutive boys, he would become a werewolf.

The action of spiritually consuming the food, drink, the blood, or the energy of people by night can also be interpreted under

88 Campagne, 'Witch or Demon? Fairies, Vampires and Nightmares in Early Modern Spain.' 381–410; 382.

89 Castell, "Wine vat witches suffocate children." The Mythical Components of the Iberian Witch." 170–195; 185-186.

90 Reguera, 'La brujería vasca en la Edad Moderna: aquelarres, hechicería y curanderismo.' 240–283: 245.

91 Ibid., 266.

92 Examples of such ristras de bautizo can be found in the Museo de Creencias y Religiosidad Popular del Pirineo in Abizanda (Aragon).

93 Campagne, 'Witch or Demon? Fairies, Vampires and Nightmares in Early Modern Spain', 381–410; 394.

the light of the dark shamanism theory by Emma Wilby (briefly outlined in the second chapter of this book). According to that theory, disembodied spirits or the manifestations of the human double could carry out the consumption or attack of those human and natural resources. We should not forget that the basis of all Pyrenean witch craze, crystalized in the Catalan *Ordinacions* law of 1424, focused on the possibility of human beings joining the retinue of spirits, *anar amb les bruxes* 'go with the bruxes.' The question is: could a human individual become a member of the night host, and become one with the *bruxes?* If so, how?

GRANTING OF POWERS
AND INITIATION RITES

*W*E proceed now to analyse beliefs about how a human individual could become part of the night army. In Pyrenean folklore, such abilities were sometimes thought to be inborn, a series of birth and early childhood conditions that enabled a person to become a *bruxa* or other supernatural being. In Aragon, it was believed that if the person were born the consecutive seventh son or daughter, he or she would become a *bruxa*,[94] as with the werewolf and the nightmare. Also, in the region of Languedoc, the date of birth could also cause a person to become a *bruxa* or an *armier*, particularly if born during All Hallow's Day or on Christmas Day. The period between All Hallows' Eve and Christmas was very important for the *armier*, being the time when the souls of the dead were thought to be the most active.[95] In the area of Montagne Noire, the 'black mountain', next to the village of Mazamet (French Pyrenees), people believed the following:

> *...les enfants qui naissent le jour d'un fait d'armes auront la faculté de faire sortir et rentrer à volonté leur âme dans le corps; ils éprou-*

94 Gari Lacruz, Ángel. *Brujería e Inquisición en Aragón*, 99.
95 Piniès, *Figures de la sorcellerie languedocienne*, 228-241.

veront le besoin de torumenter les gens pendants le sommeil; et ils devinedront sorciers sous le nom de masques.

(...children who are born during a day of battle have the faculty to allow their souls to leave and enter the body at will; they have the power to torment the sleepers, and become sorcerers under the name of *masques*.) [96]

In this case, the child would become a *masca*, a supernatural being that was sometimes regarded as a nightmare, as a sorcerer, or as a *bruxa*. Importantly enough, the same date of birth would mean a new-born child would become a werewolf or *kalikantzaroi* in Greece or Crete.[97] In some Pyrenean towns, not being properly baptised would also be considered a condition to becoming a *bruxa*.[98] Generally speaking, neither gender nor age would rule out the possibility of becoming a *bruxa* or attending the *ajunt*.[99]

Other ways to receive the power to separate the spirit Double from the body would be by being touched—even a handshake— by a former witch on his or her deathbed,[100] or receiving a piece of clothing from a former witch,[101] which, as we have seen, is a metaphor for the physical body, perhaps in this case indicating the secret key to free the Double. In Aragon, they believed that if a person received a token from a former witch, the person would become a witch as well,[102] Also, if a person stole something from the witch, the witch would lose its powers, and unless the witch got rid of his or her token, he or she would live forever.[103]

96 Piniès, *Figures de la sorcellerie languedocienne*, 49.
97 Ginzburg, *Ecstasies*, 232.
98 Barandiarán, *Brujería y brujas. Testimonios recogidos en el País Vasco*, 8.
99 Gari Lacruz, 'Brujería en Aragon', 27–44; 33.
100 Piniès, *Figures de la sorcellerie languedocienne*, 108.
101 Barandiarán, *Brujería y brujas. Testimonios recogidos en el País Vasco*, 8.
102 Gari Lacruz, *Brujería e Inquisición en Aragón*, 96.
103 Barandiarán, *Brujería y brujas. Testimonios recogidos en el País Vasco*, 106.

In other cases, the way to become a *bruxa* would be through the reception of a demon familiar. Pyrenean familiars, known as *minairons* in Catalan or *familierrak* in Basque, are spirits that help the *bruxa*, the sorcerer, and the magi in the completion of their tasks and facilitating their journey to the *ajunt*. These were often contained in rings, talismans, or in some cases, in special spirit vessels known as *canutets, kuttun* or *jostorratz*, similar to a needle case, the reception of which would also cause transformation into a *bruxa*.[104] In some Pyrenean areas, the transmission of familiar spirits was paramount in the categorisation of an individual as a *bruxa*.[105] There are a couple of cases in which the intervention of demon familiars was used as argument during witch trials in the Pyrenees. One case is that of Catalina Aznar, accused of being a *bruja* in 1511 in the Pyrenees of Aragon: she would call her demon familiar *mozo* 'handyman'.[106] In Basque folklore, familiars were often their own dead relatives, who would visit the living and consume food offerings.[107] The most popular apparition of familiar spirits as assistants to *bruxes* would be in the form of toads, as attested in the Zugarramurdi and the Andorran trials, in which attendants at the *ajunt* were given a personal toad to act as a familiar.[108] In the *auto de fe* that took place in Logroño 1610, it was said that each novice who wanted to become part of the *ajunt* was given a toad dressed in human clothes that would become "their guardian angel".[109] The toad, as we shall see, would embody a peculiar symbolism in the Pyrenean region.

Pascual Clemente was a farmer in the town of Embún (Aragonese Pyrenees), who was tried for witchcraft in 1609. Clemente told the inquisitors that he was able to harvest an enormous amount of grain thanks to the demon familiars he kept in the han-

---

104 Ibid., 8.
105 Gari Lacruz, *Brujería e Inquisición en Aragón*, 86.
106 Tausiet, *Ponzoña en los ojos. Brujería y superstición en Aragón en el siglo xvi*, 270.
107 Barandiarán, *Mitología Vasca*, 57.
108 Pastor i Castillo, *Aquí les penjaven*, 177.
109 Caro Baroja, *Las brujas y su mundo*, 228.

dle of his scythe, in the form of five grains of *yerba falaguera*.[110] To obtain these familiars, Pascual was obliged to offer his soul to the Devil and renounce his Christian faith; however, his relationship with the familiars was limited to five years, after which the pact with those demons would dissolve.[111] Perhaps the most paradigmatic case involving demon familiars is the trial against sorcerer Jerónimo de Liébana, also in Aragón in 1621. The man, pretending to be a priest, told five men he would teach them to obtain demon familiars and keep them inside a special talismanic ring that would later provide them with amazing riches and great success with women.[112]

Other ways to receive supernatural powers included offering one's shoes (especially the left one) to the Devil, either by waiting for him to present himself in the shape of a cat or by tossing them up in the air. Offering a shoe makes sense considering the folkloric image of the Devil as a limping or wooden-footed character: the potential *bruxa* or sorcerer offers a shoe to become one with the Devil, having one foot in each world. The shoe was also considered a fitting payment for the favours that the Devil had bestowed,[113] but this offering was not exclusive to the Devil. There is also evidence of left sandals being offered to Hecate in ancient times.[114] The offering of left shoes and sandals may be viewed as an initiatory symbol of death and rebirth, and the will to cross to the other side.

Initiation rituals were evidently the most widespread way to become a temporary member of the night crusade. In most Pyrenean accounts, initiation rituals happened during the *ajunt* where the individual would become a *bruxa* and assume features normally associated with the spirit Double. On some occasions, it was

---

110 Most likely henbane caps. Tausiet, *Ponzoña en los ojos. Brujería y superstición en Aragón en el siglo xvi,* 266.
111 Ibid.
112 Tausiet, *Ponzoña en los ojos. Brujería y superstición en Aragón en el siglo xvi,* 269.
113 Ibid., 12.
114 Ginzburg, *Ecstasies,* 233.

possible to become a *bruxa* by performing a series of ceremonies that, in the Basque country, included circling a church three times at midnight;[115] or, in Catalonia, wallowing naked in a patch of nettles or brambles while renouncing god. This same method was advised for those wishing to become an animal.[116] Bramble patch thorns would not harm the individual, since the physical body would still be in bed, or numbed into an unconscious state. The abilities arising from the *bruxa*'s initiation were usually time limited, during periods that ranged from four to nine years. We have found a parallel in the temporality of the familiar spirit assistance, referenced by Emma Wilby,[117] and also of werewolf states, as analysed in Carlo Ginzburg's *Ecstasies*.[118]

THE FLIGHT, THE FEAST, AND THE MISCHIEF

To offer a classical outline and subsequent analysis of the Pyrenean *ajunt de bruxes*, we will focus on the structure presented in the Zugarramudi trials, considered by most researchers the most complete account of a later medieval/Early Modern *ajunt de bruxes*.[119] Roughly speaking, the default Pyrenean *ajunt* was to occur on Monday, Wednesday, or Friday nights, principally during the festivities of Christmas, Easter, Midsummer's Eve, or during All Hallow's Eve, and these meetings would last from midnight to the dawn's rooster's crow at dawn. Before setting off to the appointed place, attendants would apply a special ointment, recite an incantation for flight, and fly to the *ajunt* through chimneys, doors, and windows. Once they arrived at the *ajunt*, they would

115 Barandiarán, José Miguel de. 2012. *Brujería y brujas. Testimonios recogidos en el País Vasco*, 8.
116 Apeles Mestres, *Llegendes i tradicions del Montseny*. In Amades, *Bruixes i bruixots*, 50.
117 Wilby, *Cunning Folk and Familiar Spirits*, 77.
118 Ginzburg, Carlo. 1990. *Ecstasies*, 135.
119 Henningsen, Gustav, *El abogado de las brujas. Brujería vasca e Inquisición Española*, 116-117.

pledge allegiance to the Devil, kissing his left hand or performing the *osculum infame*, i.e., kissing Satan's buttocks. They would
celebrate an orgiastic revelry, a feast consisting of dreadful concoctions, hideous music, macabre dances, and, sometimes, aberrant
sexual intercourse. The attendants would then be marked by the
Devil or sign their names in a special book, and given instructions
on how to spread pestilence and misfortunes to please their Master.[120] As the reader may have noticed, some of the actions present
in this brief account of the *ajunt de bruxes* have clear theological
origins from previous anti-heretical prosecutions; some have folkloric origins in European folk beliefs on the otherworld and ideas
underpinning ecstatic journeys. Our duty then, is to question each
of these and try to determine their origins.

ꟻ Preparation and Incantations

According to Pyrenean witch lore, attendants might be offered
special food to be gain access to the *ajunt*. Like Juanes de Ugarte
(Navarra), who was given some millet, or some chestnuts. Millet,
curiously enough, is commonly offered to the Dead on All Hallows
Eve in the Languedoc region.[121] Or, as happened to Catalina de
Alonso, or María Gómez, who were given fish by their mistres-
es.[122] In the Pyrenees of Aragon, Juan Larrat, tried for witchcraft,
gave a drink to a maiden, declaring that it would cause her to fall
into a deep sleep.[123] On other occasions, food and drink would be
substituted by the application of the infamous witches' ointment.
    The first mention of an ointment in relation to the *ajunt de*

---

120 The structure of the trial is outlined in the auto de fe of Logroño
     1610 and summarised in Henningsen, *El abogado de las brujas. Bru-
     jería vasca e Inquisición Española*, 116-117.
121 Piniès, *Figures de la sorcellerie languedocienne*, 212.
122 Reguera, 'La brujería vasca en la Edad Moderna: aquelarres, he-
     chicería y curanderismo', 240-283: 251.
123 Gari Lacruz, 'Los aquelarres en Aragón según los documentos y la
     tradición oral.' In *Temas de antropología aragonesa*, 4 (1993), 241-261;
     243.

bruxes appeared in the trial against Narbona Darcal, in the Pyrenees of Aragon in 1498,[124] later spreading to many other trials in
other Pyrenean territories. The initial composition of the ointment would often include poisonous plants like hellebore or aco-
nite, the ashes and fat of unbaptized babies, human bones, arsenic,
or bat's blood among other ingredients. The ointment was at that
time seen as a gift that the Devil gave to his acolytes not only to
facilitate transportation to the *ajunt*, but also to poison their neighbours and even members of their own family: one ointment could
facilitate flight, but could also kill those who were not *bruxes*.

However, mentions of the ointment stopped after 1550, when
the explanation for flight was attributed to demonic possession.
During that period, epidemic cases of possession began to appear
more frequently. The ointment and ritual ingestion of food and
drink were first replaced with the illusion of demon-driven flight
proposed by theologians, later substituted by the hallucinogenic
drug theory begun by empiricist scientists in the Early Modern
period, who claimed that the origin of the flight could be found
in the use of psychoactive substances. Again, the enlightened approach seems to discard any possibility of spirit flight being an
instance of factual contact with the Otherworld. We should remember that the actual composition of the ointment is not what
was interesting, but the belief in a tool used to numb the body
in order to allow spirit detachment. The ingestion of food and
drink or the application of an ointment, also present in fairy tales,
meant the acceptance of an otherworldly gift that allowed human
beings interaction with the *bruxes*. As brilliantly stated by Gustav
Henningsen:

> Constant reference to certain hallucinogenic ointments con-
> stitutes an ancient pseudoscientific attempt to give the phe-
> nomenon of witchcraft a rational explanation.[125]

124 Gari Lacruz, Ángel. 2010. 'Brujería en los Pirineos (siglos xiii al
xvii). Aproximación a su historia', 317–354; 331.

125 Henningsen, *El abogado de las brujas. Brujería vasca e Inquisición Espa-*

While it is undeniable that some of the plants mentioned in ointment recipes would have an undoubtable effect on the psyche and
the body, some of those plants had already been used in medicine
for centuries, and part of its inclusion in ointment recipes was motivated by an increasing suspicion against folk medicine and folk
magic as well as against *metzineria/ponzoñería/veneficium*, which
rapidly merged with the new crime of witchcraft. The witches'
ointment, whose concept, let's not forget, originated in the prosecution against heretic groups, is not to be found in science but in
mysticism.

Another significant device in preparation for the sabbatical
journey were flight incantations; Pyrenean flight incantations are
especially peculiar. Most can be categorised into two typologies:
incantations including some sort of blasphemy, and incantations
mentioning thorns or hedge plants. In the first typology we can
find examples, such as in the 1610 Zugarramurdi case:

*Yo soy demonio / Yo de aquí adelante tengo de ser una misma cosa con
el Demonio / Yo he de ser demonio / y no he de tener nada con Dios.*

(I am demon / From now on I am one with the Devil / I have
to be a demon / and have nothing to do with God.)[126]

The incantation displays a blasphemous taboo, i.e., the person is
no longer a person, but has transformed into a demon, united with
the Devil. Another instance of blasphemous flight incantations is
found in the 1540 trial against some women in Ochagavía (Navarra): *la hizo renegar de Dios y de Santa María y de todos sus santos,
y de los genollos de su padre y tetas de su madre,* ("the Devil made her
renounce God, the Virgin Mary, and all the saints, the genitalia of
his father, and the breasts of her mother.")[127] A similar incantation

---

ñola, 455.

126 Ibid., 116.

127 Gari Lacruz, 'Brujería en los Pirineos (siglos xiii al xvii). Aproxi-
     mación a su historia' 317–354; 339.

would appear in Tamarite (Aragonese Pyrenees) in 1626: *Renegar de Dios, del padre que los engendró y de la madre que los parió* ("Deny god, the father that spawned them and the mother who gave them birth").[128] According to Angel Gari, this type of flight incantation was seen as an offence to all the symbols of power, represented by one's god, father, and mother. Denying all three of them would imply renouncing everything sacred.[129]

Let us now focus on the second type of Pyrenean incantations, those mentioning thorns and hedges. Instances of such flight incantations are found as early as 1471 and 1484, in the processes against the alleged Catalan *bruxes* Margarida Anglada from Mosquera, and Valentina Guarner. The written account of their trials states that they uttered the following formula before flying to the *Lana del Boc* 'the Land of the Goat': *Pich sobre fulla, que vagi allà on vulla*, 'thorn/bush over leaf, I shall go wherever I please'.[130] This same formula stood the test of time and moved throughout other Pyrenean territories. It was collected in the *Llibre Blanc d'Occitaine* in 1555, a compendium of laws and customs from the area, where the spell appeared in the form *pet sus fuèlha*.[131] It also appeared in Pierre de Lancre's 1612 *Tableau de l'inconstance des mauvais anges et démons*. Here, De Lancre quoted the testimony provided by Estebene de Cambrue who claimed that the witches of Amou (French Pyrenees) uttered this before meeting at the designated place, where "they danced around a standing stone which was planted at the site on top of which sat a black man." The formula used in that case was: *Pic suber hoeilha, enta la lane de bouc bien m'arrecouille*[132]

128 Gari Lacruz, 'Brujería en Aragon', 27-44: 36.

129 Ibid., 27-44: 36.

130 Anglada 1471, a Castell, *Orígens i evolució de la cacera de bruixes a Catalunya (segles XV–XVI)*, 88.

131 Piniès, "Pet-sus-fuelha ou le depart des sorciers pour le sabbat," 247-266.

132 Pierre de Lancre, *Le Tableau de L'inconstance des Mauvais Anges et Démons où il est amplement traicté de la sorcellerie et sorciers*, livre II, discours 4, a Nicolas Ghersi, 'Poisons, sorcières et lande de bouc', *Cahiers de recherches médiévales*, 17 (2009): 103-120; p. 119.

'thorn/bush over leaf, may the land of the goat take hold of me'. Finally, a slight variation of the spell made it through the 19th century to be found in a tale told in Berga (Catalan Pyrenees), collected by folklorist Cels Gomis in which a *bruxa*, after turning its husband into an ass, said *Per damunt fulla, a Pedraforca*[133] 'Over leaf, to Pedraforca', and went into the air riding its husband-donkey to attend the nocturnal gathering.

In Aragon, the *pic i fulla* incantation would suffer a series of modifications. Its first example dates from the process against Narbona Darcal in 1498, only twenty years after the first *pich i fulla* incantations were recorded in Catalonia. The accused claimed that, after anointing herself with the ointment, she spoke the spell aloud and flew through the air towards the Land of the Goat. *Sobre arto y sobre espina a lanna de boch siamos ayna,*[134] 'Over buckthorn and over thorn (bush), we make haste to the land of the goat.' This same Aragonese flight incantation was used for two centuries, found even in the process against the witches of Fago in 1657.[135] It must be added that *arto* is a word used in the area of Aragon to designate thorny bushes such as hawthorn, buckthorn and blackthorn, and the *espina*, meaning 'thorn', is strongly related to Pyrenean plant folklore. Thorn bushes and brambles are widely used in the Pyrenees for their magical and medicinal properties, and they all share the ability to generate hedges, enclosing the plot of land in both the physical and symbolic senses.

The most popular version of flight incantation in the Basque country, collected in legends and other trials, also mention thorny bushes, reminding us of their relevance in Pyrenean folklore: *Sasi guztien gaiñetik eta laiño guztien azpitik*[136] 'Above the brambles and below the clouds.' Thorn bushes of several varieties but specially

---

133 Gomis, *La bruixa catalana,* 57.

134 Gari Lacruz, 'Brujería en los Pirineos (siglos xiii al xvii). Aproximación a su historia.' 317–354; 331.

135 Ibid.

136 Story told by Zubillaga Galarza, April 26th in Garmendia de Larrañaga. *Sorginak, akerra eta lapurrak.* Pointed by María Martínez Pisón through written correspondence.

hawthorn, briar rose, and brambles, were commonly used in the Pyrenees as amulets against the attack of *bruxes*, and to prevent storms from damaging the crops. Also, as we have mentioned earlier in this chapter, the initiatory rite of wallowing naked in a patch of brambles and avoiding damage is also especially relevant in this case. Again, it seems that the goal of such formulae was to create a barrier between the two worlds that only *bruxes* can trespass.

The final example of a flight incantation we analyse in this chapter dates from 1534, found in the Aragonese Pyrenees in the trial against Dominica la Coja:[137] *fulla sobre fulla a las Eras de Tolosa sea luego allá,* ("Leaf over leaf in the fields of Tolosa I shall quickly appear"). Like other instances of Pyrenean flight incantations, the gathering place mentioned in this spell (the eras de Tolosa) is the Aragonese equivalent to the 'land of the goat', which we discussed in the previous chapter. Some authors, like María Tausiet, argue that the mention of Tolosa, a Spanish translation of Toulouse, capital city of the Occitan region, could refer to the theological idea of *ajunt* being born in that region after the anti-heretical crusade.[138] Again, it's an undetermined place in the Pyrenean geography, a dream landmark that may only be reached through the transformative process of going with the *bruxes*.

In many Pyrenean folktales, flight incantations are displayed as keys that can only be understood by the initiated or by those ready to commence the journey towards the Land of the Goat. This is why we find many tales where an external observer spies upon a *bruxa* getting ready to attend the *ajunt* and wanting to follow her, he utters a mistaken version of the incantation with dramatic results. Perhaps the most famous example is the Basque version of the tale: an orphan boy discovers that his grandmother is a sorgin, and he spies her one night while she enunciates the incantation *Sasi guztien gaiñetik eta laiño guztien azpitik* ("Above the brambles and below the clouds"), before heading to the *ajunt*. The boy tries

137 Gari Lacruz, 'La brujería en los Pirineos (ss. XIII–XVIII). Una aproximación a su historia', 333.
138 Tausiet, *Ponzoña en los ojos,* 280.

to imitate his grandmother but mixing it up, he instead says 'underneath the brambles and over the clouds', resulting in the boy painfully passing through the bramble bushes.[139]

Thorns, leaves, and brambles are liminal elements which guide us in crossing the frontiers between worlds; they are the Keys to the *ajunt*, guardians of the path that leads us to meet *bruxa*. Powerful brambles and their thorns separate those willing to sacrifice their flesh and blood from those who fear pain and dare not participate. That could be the reason behind cautionary tales such as the one referred above: only those individuals who know the precise incantation—or the ones who can understand it—will be able to go through the Ordeal of Thorns, while those who are still human will not be able to bear the agony of such a transformative experience. This shall be explored further in investigating the witches' inability to feel pain as part of the gifts and teachings bestowed by the Devil.

After the ointment and the incantation, the flight would take place. In most accounts and trials, the sensation of flight is described as similar to a dream or drowsy state. Such a feeling was narrated in 1534 by the accused Gabriel Mora, a man from the Catalan village of Estac, who described all sorts of fantastic events happening in the *ajunt de bruixes*.[140] Similar can be found in the testimonies of individuals tried at Zugarramurdi, who claimed they could not hear nor see anything during the journey, and that they were not missed at home. Quoting one of the accused, called Juanes de Ugarte:

> *que aunque lloviese o nevase éste nunca se mojó ni sintió ruido de perros ni otros animales, ni tocar campanas, ni ha visto a otras personas más de los que son brujos.*[141]

139 This tale was told by Josefa Zubillaga Galarza to Juan Garmendia Larrañaga in 1981. Juan Garmendia Larrañaga, "Sorginak, akerra eta lapurrak", *Eusko Ikaskuntza* (2007), 13–14.

140 Castell, *Orígens i evolució de la cacera de bruixes a Catalunya*, 92.

141 Reguera, 'La brujería vasca en la Edad Moderna: aquelarres, he-

(That although it rained or it snowed he never got wet, nor did he hear noises from dogs or other animals, nor the toll of the bells, and he didn't see anyone who weren't *brujos* there.)

It seems as though the accused described a dream or trance-like experience not observable in the tangible world, but was completely real to them.

THE FEAST

𝕬 FTER the ointment and the journey, attendants would typically arrive in the Land of the Goat and engage in the orgiastic feast. Supernatural entities and *bruxes* would often attend the feast, sometimes accompanied by their spirit familiars, all presided over by the Devil. However, in some cases the Devil would also have to share his ruling position with a certain woman dressed in green mentioned in some Basque testimonies, as in 1575 by María Hernandoiz, who claimed:

> *Y la otra figura era como de mujer que estaba asentada en la dicha silla con parecer hermoso y blanco y vestida de verde con rostro, manos y pies de mujer.*

(And the other figure looked like a woman who was sitting on a chair, beautiful and pale, and she was dressed in green, with a woman's face, hands, and feet.)[142]

The Devil would receive each attendant, who would kiss him in reverence, reaffirming fidelity and abjuring the Christian faith re-

---

chicería y curanderismo.', 253.

142 Usunáriz Garayoa, *La caza de brujas en la Navarra moderna (siglos XVI–XVII) Rev. int. estud. vascos. Cuad., 9, 306-350: pp. 323-325 in* Gari Lacruz, 'Brujería en los Pirineos (siglos xiii al xvii). Aproximación a su historia.' In *Cuadernos de etnología y etnografía de Navarra*, año 42, no. 85, 317-354; 339.

nouncing god, Jesus, and the Virgin Mary.[143] Furthermore, as part of the blasphemous activities that conformed the *ajunt*, followers would perform the *osculum infame*, which was recorded for the first time in trials against the Templars and other heretical orders.[144]

The consumption of food and drink in the sabbatic feast indicates, as it did in preparation for the gathering, the otherworldly dimension of the event. Those accused of witchcraft would often describe food that could not be actually eaten, or food in quantities that never diminished. Some attendants claimed that they pretended to eat, or that the food would disappear while they were eating, as if they ate only air.[145] Catalina de Guesala, a woman who underwent trial for attending the *ajunt* of Ceberio (Basque Country) said that *hicieron como que comían y les daba de beber en una taza grande que parecía de plata*, 'they pretended to eat, and they were given to drink out from a big cup that looked as if it were made of silver'.[146]

On other occasions, the food would be good and plentiful. Margarida Anglada (Catalan Pyrenees) claimed during her trial that there was cheese, bread, meat, and wine, and even fruit.[147] In other testimonies, the food would be far from pleasing, as part of necrophagous and cannibalistic activities. The flesh of dead people

---

143 Henningsen, *El abogado de las brujas. Brujería vasca e Inquisición Española*, 116–117.

144 Cohn, *Europe's Inner Demons: The Demonization of Christians in Medieval Christendom*, 43.

145 In some cases, the food disappears when they eat it. Reguera, 'La brujería vasca en la Edad Moderna: aquelarres, hechicería y curanderismo.' In *Rev. int. estud. vascos*. Cuaderno 9: 240–283: 261.

146 Ibid.

147 Castell, *Orígens i evolució de la cacera de bruixes a Catalunya*, 90. As stated by Emma Wilby: "Sweet smells and tastes are frequently recorded by contemplatives who reach high stages of meditation. The anonymous author of The Cloud of Unknowing, with characteristic austerity, warns that such experiences are distractions created by the Devil and should be guarded against." *Cunning Folk and Familiar Spirits: Shamanistic Visionary Traditions in Early Modern British Witchcraft and Magic*, 292, n. 77.

would be served, even that of a member of one's own family.[148] In
the trials of Bermeo, (Navarra), boys who testified as witnesses at a
witch trial said that attendants were fed "the flesh of dead witches,
bitter, reeking, (...) black bread, and black drinks, but they did
nothing but chew that because the food would disappear from
their mouths and they could not swallow it".[149] Catalina Fernández de Lecea said that in the *ajunt*, "they would eat meat from
people they killed (...) and they went to the churchyard and dug
up bodies from their graves, and took them to the *ajunt* where they
would roast them and boil them in pieces",[150] an account repeated
in several occasions to even include the consumption of flesh from
other dead witches:

> ...*ponen unas mesas grandes y se sientan y comen en ellas un pan ne-
> gro y carne asquerosa y hedionda negra y colorada que dicen ser de
> las brujas muertas que suelen desenterrar de las iglesias y sepulturas
> (...) y pan sin sal y agua dulce.*

(They set big tables and sit and eat in them black bread,
reeking black and red meat which they say comes from dead
witches that they dug up from churchyards and graves...and
saltless bread and sweet water.)[151]

The ingestion of food and drink, whether real or unreal, pleasant or disgusting, symbolises a ceremony of communion with the
supernatural and intangible beings in the *ajunt*. This again bears
a strong resemblance with European fairy tales in which the protagonist finds himself at a fantastical feast. The food and drink
that the attendant consumes, disobeying a folklore rule according

148 Henningsen, *El abogado de las brujas. Brujería vasca e Inquisición Española*, 130.
149 Reguera, 'La brujería vasca en la Edad Moderna: aquelarres, hechicería y curanderismo', 240-283: 261.
150 Ibid., 240-283: p. 261.
151 Ibid.

to which one must never eat the food given by fairies, makes him or her one with the hosts, and is finally denied the ability to return to the tangible world again.[152] Another common factor in the *ajunt de bruxes* is the absence of salt, being a preservative, i.e., preventing rot and decomposition. In this case, saltless food is meant to be spoiled, it is meant to be consumed by spirits.[153]

The feast was followed by a frenetic dance, usually to the sound of traditional instruments, and a wild orgy in which people perform sinful actions. Sexual intercourse would often occur both among the attendants and with the Devil. However, allusion to sexual intercourse would diminish in the first half of the 16th century, when sex was replaced with other blasphemous, yet less controversial, activities like trodding upon the cross.[154] Testimonies claimed that the attendants, both women and men, were often sodomised, as in the case of Gabriela Sansi from Esterri d'Àneu in 1592, or the case of Gabriel Móra from Estac in 1534 who, together with the other attendants of the *ajunt*, found the Devil *en forma de un boch*, "in the shape of a goat" and after pledging their allegiance to him, *ell ens ho féu a tots per detràs* ("he sodomised us all").[155]

Attendants sometimes described intercourse as painful, as the Devil had a cold[156] or thorny[157] penis. Mari Hernández, for example, was "corrupted" by the devil under the name *Belzebut*, losing her virginity and returning home with a bloody shirt.[158] However, it seems pertinent to state that the idea of painful intercourse with

152 Holger Kalweit, *Dreamtime & Inner Space: The World of the Shaman*, in Wilby, *Cunning Folk and Familiar Spirits: Shamanistic Visionary Traditions in Early Modern British Witchcraft and Magic*, 85.

153 Further information in Daniel Schulke, *Veneficium* (2012), 82-84.

154 Castell, *Orígens i evolució de la cacera de bruixes a Catalunya*, 91.

155 Castell, *Un Judici a la Terra dels Bruixots. La Cacera de bruixes a la Vall Fosca 1548-1549*, 33.

156 Scott E. Hendrix, 'The Pursuit of Witches and the Sexual Discourse of the Sabbat,' 41-59: 55.

157 Marliave, *Dictionnaire de magie et de sorcellerie dans les Pyrénées*, 274.

158 Usunáriz Garayoa, 'La caza de brujas en la Navarra moderna (siglos XVI-XVII).' 323-325: 325.

the Devil and reference to his unusual genitalia possibly appeared for the first time in the *Vox in rama* bull, a religious text promulgated in 1233 by Pope Gregory IX while prosecuting German heretics.[159] Nevertheless, on other occasions the intercourse was pleasurable, as in the case of Jeannette d'Abadie, who testified in front of Pierre de Lancre that intercourse with the Devil had been delightful as his penis had *belle forme et mesure,* 'beautiful shape and measure'.[160] In other occasions, sexual intercourse would be economically rewarded. We find in the 1498 trial against Narbona Darcal:

> *...en donde estava el boch de Biterna, al qual todas besaban en el trasero y lo honrravan y adoravan, y se echava con ellas y las estrenava, y les dava en pago ciertos dineros, y baliavan y se solaçavan allí, en el dicho campo...*

> (...where the boch de Biterna appeared, everyone kissed him on the back and honoured and worshipped him, he would lay down and corrupt them, he would pay them in return with some money, and they danced and enjoyed themselves in that field...)[161]

This was not the only example of the Devil paying in exchange for the sexual services of witches, as also happened with Mari Hernández, who was given a 'coin that looked like gold'.[162]

Some Pyrenean folktales and legends tell us how, in some exceptional cases, a person who wasn't supposed to be there accessed the *ajunt de bruxes.* The person would discover the *ajunt* and pronounce the name of god, Jesus, or the Virgin Mary, or make the

159 Castell, *Orígens i evolució de la cacera de bruixes a Catalunya,* 65.
160 Marliave, *Dictionnaire de magie et de sorcellerie dans les Pyrénées,* 274.
161 Tausiet, *Ponzoña en los ojos. Brujería y superstición en Aragón en el siglo xvi,* 279.
162 Usunáriz Garayoa, 'La caza de brujas en la Navarra moderna (siglos XVI–XVII).' 306–350: 323–325.

sign of the cross, wreaking havoc. In those cases, the entire gathering and its attendants would just disappear.[163] This idea would survive in Pyrenean folktales, as one from Ayerbe in the Pyrenees of Aragon,[164] or a more complete example in the Basque country, in a story told by a shepherd who saw strange lights and discovered some people he recognized as his neighbours. Amazed, he began making the sign of the cross while pronouncing the name of Jesus, to suddenly appear in the middle of nowhere.[165] Pronouncing holy names or making the sign of the cross would be seen as an attack to the heretic and demonic character of the reunion, and would immediately dissolve it.

As we have seen, the Pyrenean *ajunt de bruxes* displays a series of elements that could be attributed to the prosecution of heretics: the *osculum infame*, and other blasphemous activities like stepping on the cross or signing the Devil's book, refusing to pronounce the name of god, and the celebration of sinful orgies.[166] Those diabolic aspects of witchcraft emerged from an anti-heretic discourse, presumably in Southern France, where the prosecution against heretic groups had persisted since the 12th century.[167] Heretical elements, however, would disappear after the witch craze, while the purposes of the original actions attributed to the primordial *bruxes*—crushing sleepers, killing children and cattle, creating storms, administering *metzines* and *mal donat* — would stand the test of time, following a customary belief deeply rooted in mountain communities.

163 Ibid., 306-350: 323-325.
164 Gari Lacruz, 'Los aquelarres en Aragón según los documentos y la tradición oral', 241-261; 251.
165 Reguera, 'La brujería vasca en la Edad Moderna: aquelarres, hechicería y curanderismo,' 240-283, 264-265.
166 Castell, *Un Judici a la Terra dels Bruixots. La Cacera de bruixes a la Vall Fosca 1548-1549*, 34.
167 Tausiet, *Ponzoña en los ojos. Brujería y superstición en Aragón en el siglo xvi*, 277.

AN ART OF THE DEVIL

𝕬 TTENDANTS of the *ajunt de bruxes* did not return home emp-ty-handed. In most cases, they had been marked, taught, or compelled by their Master to spread his will. Results of attending the *ajunt* would be made evident in their ways, in their spirits, and their bodies. Some signs indicating that a person had attended the *ajunt* were evident in the attendees' behaviour, like Valentina Guarner, who was unable to see the holy wafer at mass: all she

saw was a black shape.[168] The same happened in the Basque country and in Navarra,[169] where *ajunt* attendants could see neither the
holy wafer nor the holy chalice. Nonetheless, the most famous
evidence of allegiance with the Devil and attendance to the *ajunt*
manifested in the attendants' bodies: the infamous Mark of the
Devil, and the witches' inability to feel pain. The Mark of the
Devil is a complex topic, as it seems to suggest the merging of
two ideas: one can be read as a concept originating in theological
spheres as judicial evidence to be sought in trials. However, the
Devil's Mark and an inability to cry could also be seen as an indica-
tion of the non-humanity of the attendant. In Pyrenean witchcraft,
the Mark of the Devil was normally found on the left side of the
body,[170] mainly on the shoulder or left eye.[171] The shape of the
mark would also depend on the time and place of the testimony,
but often included marks taking the shape of the foot of a toad,[172]
hare, rabbit,[173] or hen.[174]

It does not seem coincidental to see the toad mentioned again.
When looking at the symbolic significance of the toad in certain
Pyrenean regions, Basque and Navarra in particular, we find the
toad is traditionally regarded as the "worst animal" in nature, and
bearing the mark of the toad on the eye would be a sign of the
iniquity and wickedness of its bearer.[175] In some trials, it was said
that a malefic magician would *zapoaren eskua ezkier begian* ("have

168   Padilla Lapuente, *L'esperit d'Àneu: llibre dels costums i ordinacions de les
      Valls d'Àneu,* 1999.

169   Caro Baroja, *Brujería vasca,* 32.

170   Reguera, 'La brujería vasca en la Edad Moderna: aquelarres, he-
      chicería y curanderismo', 240-283: 256.

171   Henningsen, *El abogado de las brujas. Brujería vasca e Inquisición Espa-
      ñola,* 121.

172   Caro Baroja, *Brujería vasca,* 71.

173   Horace Chauvet, *Legendes du Roussillon,* (1899), 35. In Amades, *Bruix-
      es i bruixots,* 50.

174   Tausiet *Ponzoña en los ojos. Brujería y superstición en Aragón en el siglo xvi,*
      335.

175   Azurmendi, *Nombrar, embrujar. Para una historia del sometimiento de la
      cultura oral en el País Vasco,* 182-184.

the power of the toad in one's left eye"): having evil in one's eye or having the capacity to give the evil eye.[176] The idea of the toad as an evil animal was already present in the aforementioned papal bull *Vox in rama*, in which the Devil is often referred to as a toad that must be kissed on the mouth or on the buttocks.[177] *Bruxes* and *fetillers* were considered able to perform magic and administer *metzines* because of the toad foot mark on their eyes, as it was through the eye that they performed *mau dat* or *mal donat*, 'maleficium'. This would explain reference in the Aragonese Pyrenees to the ability to perform harmful magic as *tener ponzoña en los ojos:* "to have poison in one's eyes".[178] In fact, the Basque synonym for *bruxa* is often *belagile,* which would stand for 'person who looks at someone to wish him or her evil.'[179] Also the toad was regarded as the emblematic familiar to Basque *sorginak*, and would be given special treatment during the celebration. According to some Basque testimonies, children abducted and taken to the ajunt did not always become victims to the *sorgin*'s cannibal appetite, but helped tend the toads, feeding them. Additionally, children would also take care of the bonfires, gathering wood. They might even play ball games, as it was said in the trials happening in the towns of Bermeo and Fuenterrabía, in Navarra, in the beginning of the 17th century.[180]

The Witches' mark could be administered by the Devil during a ceremony, or in a birthmark caused, according to belief, by a pregnant mother's profuse ingestion of blackberries, resulting in the new-born child bearing a red birthmark that the Devil would

176 Ibid., 184.
177 Norman Cohn, *Europe's Inner Demons: The Demonization of Christians in Medieval Christendom,* 44–49 and 76.
178 Tausiet, *Ponzoña en los ojos. Brujería y superstición en Aragón en el siglo xvi*, 30.
179 Azurmendi, *Nombrar, embrujar. Para una historia del sometimiento de la cultura oral en el País Vasco,* 189.
180 Reguera, 'La brujería vasca en la Edad Moderna: aquelarres, hechicería y curanderismo', 240–283: 262.

later use to find his acolytes.[181] That a physical mark was a sign of belonging to the *ajunt de bruxes* would be proven by its insensitivity to pain, i.e., the accused would not notice the mark being pricked. If such a spot was found during trial, it would mean the accused was in league with the Devil. Pierre De Lancre, for instance, insisted on looking for the Mark of the Devil with the aid of the *punctum diabolum*, a large iron needle employed to find a special spot in the body that could not bleed or hurt when pricked.[182] This procedure was actually carried out with the accused called Jeanette de Belloc in front of the local authorities with the aid of a foreign surgeon. It seems the girl had a mark on her skin that was totally insensitive to the *punctum,* which resulted in the girl being executed.[183]

Because *bruxes* were traditionally believed to be unable to feel pain or sadness, many Pyrenees regions claimed that hellfire could not burn them,[184] and that they were incapable of crying.[185] In some Aragonese trials, such inability to cry was actually used as judicial proof of their contact with the Devil:

> *Que despues de presa, ni hasta aora, no ha echado lagrima alguna con verse en poder de un verdugo que le reconocio, y un zirujano que le traveso la espalda, indicios todos que la convencen de hechizera...*[186]

181   María Martínez Pisón, 'Landare folklorea Nafarroako Pirinioetan.' *Por encima de Todas las Zarzas* (September 2018). https://porencimadetodaslaszarzas.com/2018/09/03/landare-folklorea-nafarroako-pirinioetan/

182   Caro Baroja, *Brujería vasca*, 204.

183   Duché-Gavet, Véronique: *Les sorcières de Pierre de Lancre* (2012) 140-155, 150.

184   Caro Baroja, *Brujería vasca*, 256.

185   Amades, *Bruixes i bruixots,* 85.

186   Tausiet, *Ponzoña en los ojos. Brujería y superstición en Aragón en el siglo xvi,* 334.

(That after being taken prisoner, and not even now, she has not shed a tear even with being in the company of an executioner who recognised her and a surgeon who picked her back, all them being signs that convince us that she is a sorceress...)

This theory was also present in the 1534 trial against Dominica la Coja, whose eyes were examined by prosecutors in search of tears, but found none.[187] Lack of pain or the inability to cry would also confirm the nature of a *bruxa* as a non-human being, and so unable to display human emotions like pain or sadness. That these signs were given paramount importance in confessions also supports the theory that witchcraft was performed only by the spiritual double. The testimony given by 14-year old Xacobe de Estacona, at her trial in Fuenterrabia (Navarra) in 1611, illustrates the dreadful incident that she endured during the *ajunt*:

No quiso renegar de dios la echaron ecima de unas aliagas y la azo-taron con un espino negro en las partes bajas. Luego la hicieron renegar a la fuerza y el diablo la selló con una marca caliente en el cuello, marca que por el momento no le causó dolor pero que al volver a casa se lo produjo y muy vivo.[188]

(She did not want to deny God so they threw her on some thorny bushes and whipped her genitalia with blackthorn branches. Then they made her deny it by force, and the Devil signalled her with a hot mark on her neck, a mark that for the moment did not cause her pain but that when she returned home it hurt her very much.)

Unwillingly, Xacobe has given us the keys to defining the gift of witchcraft: the state of the *bruxa* is temporary. The inability to feel pain perhaps only takes place during the nocturnal encounter,

187 Ibid., 335.
188 Caro Baroja, *Brujería vasca*, 239.

proving that the experience can occur only while the spirit double is out of the body.

After the *ajunt de bruxes* had ended, the attendants would have gained knowledge imparted by the Devil in ways to harm or poison people through *mau dat, begizko, maldau, mal donat,* or 'evil eye', through the instruction and preparation of *metzines* or *ponzoñas* 'poisons', by spreading epidemics, attacking people in their sleep,[189] killing or harming domestic animals, and prompting bad weather.[190] The knowledge attendants were granted had to be employed in evil doings. and if they failed to do so, there would be severe punishment.[191] Firstly, *mal donat, maldau, begizko,* or *mau dat* could be transmitted through touch, giving someone a cursed piece of food, or *mal bocí* ('bad bite',) or by taking someone's possessions, particularly clothes, hair, or nail clippings.[192]

The Devil would instruct the attendants in methods for crafting *metzines* and *ponzoñas*, the plants and substances which they would skillfully turn into poisons. The ingredients of the *metzines*—often administered in powdered form—would be *sapos, culebras, lagartos, salamandras, lagartijas, babosas, caracoles y pedos de lobo* (toads, snakes, lizards, salamanders, geckos, slugs, snails, and puffballs [*lycoperdon* spp.]).[193] The ingredients for those powders, often kept in a toad-skin pouch,[194] would be harvested in nearby fields and mountains and concocted with the help of the Devil, who would impart his blessings during the crafting process by saying *Polvos, polvos, polvos*

189 Ibid., 114.

190 Campagne, 'Witch or Demon? Fairies, Vampires and Nightmares in Early Modern Spain.' In *Acta Ethnographica Hungarica. An International Journal of Ethnography,* 53: pp. 381-410: p. 383.

191 Norman Cohn, *Europe's Inner Demons: The Demonization of Christians in Medieval Christendom,* 140.

192 Castell, *Se'n parlave…i n'hi havie. Bruixeria al Pirineu i a les terres de Ponent,* 80; Marliave, *Dictionnaire de magie et de sorcellerie dans les Pyrénées,* 221-223.

193 Henningsen, *El abogado de las brujas. Brujería vasca e Inquisición Española,* 132.

194 Caro Baroja, *Brujería vasca,* 114.

y ponzoñas ("powders, powders, powders and poisons").[195] (Poisons could be administered to sleepers at night, but would mostly be introduced in pieces of food, like el *mal bocí*,[196] introduced in bread or fruit.[197] Until recently, there were spells used to remove witches from food, such as making the sign of the cross on bread before cutting it.[198] Those *metzines* could be used to harm and kill people, or to damage the crops and spread epidemics among cattle. These concoctions were also used to spoil crops and waste grain in the same manner as when employed on people:

Cuando los campos estaban repletos de mieses maduras, (...), el demonio tomaba un puñado de polvos con la mano izquierda y los arrojaba hacia atrás diciendo: "Polvos, polvos, piérdase todo" (o "piérdase la mitad", según la magnitud de la venganza deseada). Mientras arrojaban sus polvos, los brujos repetían las palabras del diablo y añadían: «salvo sea lo mío» (...)[199]

(When the fields were ready to be harvested... the demon would take a handful of powders with his left hand and threw them backwards saying: "powders, powders, may everything be wasted away" [or "may the half be wasted", depending on the magnitude of the desired revenge]. While they threw their dusts, the sorcerers repeated the words said by the Devil and added: "except from my crops" (...).

---

195 Henningsen, *El abogado de las brujas. Brujería vasca e Inquisición Española,* 130-131.

196 Marliave, *Dictionnaire de magie et de sorcellerie dans les Pyrénées,* 312.

197 *María de Belzunegui (de Egózcue) "le quiso dar (...) una manzana colorada y muy linda y no la quiso tomar y le hizo echar de la mano y nunca más pudo haber la dicha manzana y en ello presumió que le quería dar alguna ponzoña".* Usunáriz Garayoa, "La caza de brujas en la Navarra moderna (siglos XVI-XVII)." 306-350: pp. 323-325.

198 Amades, *El Mal Donat,* 58.

199 Henningsen, *El abogado de las brujas. Brujería vasca e Inquisición Española,* 135.

The ancient link between bruxes, the Devil, and bad weather was kept alive until very recently; the belief that storms and bad weather were brought by the Devil or by a *bruxa* survived in some Pyrenean areas, seen in a 1935 testimony from the Catalan Pyrenees, according to which they believed that "ahead of storms and bad-looking clouds, there is a *bruxa* in the shape of a bird of prey that leads the wickedness of the storm."[200] The survival of the belief that connected *bruxes* and bad weather was so strong that in the Catalan Pyrenees, storms are still called *bruixonada* or *calabruix*,[201] along with the belief that each hailstone contained the hair of a goat.[202] The link between *bruxes* and bad weather was also made evident with the presence of *exconjuraderos, conjuratories*, or *comunidors*.[203] Only special healers and priests were in charge of conjuring and exorcising storms with proceedings including prayer and ritual actions, i.e. cutting the clouds with a special knife or asperging the skies with healing herbs,[204] a series of magical actions that persisted until the 1900s.[205]

Other powers attributed to *bruxes* and sorcerers gained through attendance at the *ajunt* also included the gift of dominion over animals, hence the role of the wolf-tamer or wolf-whisperer, known as *encortador de llops* in Catalan or *meneur de loups* in French. There was a 17th century case of a woman tried for witchcraft in Andorra who was said to have the power to command wolves and bears. [206] The role of the *encortador de llops*, usually linked to that of the sorcerer,[207] would continue to be practised as a quite popular branch of folk magic in some Pyrenean communities. However,

---

200 Pau Castell Granados, (ed.), *Se'n parlave...i n'hi havie. Bruixeria al Pirineu i a les terres de Ponent* (2019), 82.
201 Marliave, *Dictionnaire de magie et de sorcellerie dans les Pyrénées*, 73.
202 Ibid., 82.
203 Marliave, *Dictionnaire de magie et de sorcellerie dans les Pyrénées*, 103–104.
204 Ibid., 107.
205 Ibid., 244.
206 Ibid., 223-224.
207 Piniès, *Figures de la sorcellerie languedocienne*, p. 89.

witches' and sorcerers' powers over animals focused not only on their control over them but also on their ability to transform other people into animals. In Espinavessa (Catalan Pyrenees), for example, it was believed that sleeping husbands could be turned into donkeys to ride to the *ajunt*.[208]

The Devil granted the attendants of the *ajunt de bruxes* the mysteries of poisons and medicines, a knowledge accessed only after initiation or ritual teaching, after which followers would be conceded the knowledge of Nature, being a hostile and sinful dominion. Such experience would eventually crystallise into the elusive concept of the witches' flying ointment which, rather than attempt to discuss and deconstruct its composition as an actual concoction of herbs and other natural or supernatural substances, is better viewed as a key bearing the real mystery that prompts the journey to the *ajunt*. As a Catalan testimony from the 20th century wisely said: *if knowing metzines were indeed an art, it was an art of the Devil rather than of god.*[209]

The differentiation between folk healing practices and knowledge of poisons or *metzines* was not always clear. When the *curandero* Juan Urliac was tried for witchcraft, his ability to perform healing ceremonies was believed to be granted by the Devil, however, he claimed that what he actually did was to fight demonic forces when healing a person, and that his power came not from the devil but from god.[210] The differentiation between *curanderos*, *hechiceros*, and *bruxes* was particularly encouraged after the witch-hunt. Nowadays, the number of folk healers and folk herbalists in the Pyrenees has dramatically decreased, but once they were community resources used to solve and restore balance with the tools they had available: plant allies, animal allies, ceremonies, magical actions, etc. *Curanderos* were obviously under suspicion during the

208 Gomis, *La bruixa catalana,* 54.
209 Castell *Se'n parlave... i n'hi havie. Bruixeria al Pirineu i a les terres de Ponent*, 136.
210 Tausiet *Ponzoña en los ojos. Brujería y superstición en Aragón en el siglo xvi*, 271.

time of the witch-hunt, and often tried for their activities based on their potential to commit errors. Nonetheless, most healers claimed that their primary goal was to expel *bruxes*, preventing them from entering the body and the household, understanding them as intangible, reckless forces and bringers of maladies. The need for professional healers who understood the importance of magical protection in a community would finally surpass enmity towards those individuals potentially practising witchcraft or worshipping the Devil. The taboo of naming them as *bruxes*, however, would remain in those communities until the late 20th century, when the emergence of the New Age led to sanitising the idea of the witch, presenting them as wise men and women.

THE ORGY

THE nocturnal *ajunt* was usually said to be a fearsome, horrifying experience, although some described it as pleasant, even delightful, reminding them of paradise.[211] The accused Catalina Fernández de Lecea affirmed during her 1612 trial in the Navarrese town of Araya that she was taken to the *ajunt* by her mistress, who promised that she would enjoy herself and witness "many wonderful and pleasurable things".[212] The pleasures experienced at the *ajunt* should not be confused with the enjoyment of a holiday ritual celebration. Feasts and orgies carried out in the tangible world—collective rituals or celebrations of the natural cycles—are conducted to perpetuate the favour of deities and benefactor spirits with offerings given by human communities, part of what is known as the *economy of the sacred*,[213] especially relevant during times of epidemics, hunger, or war. The levels of excess reached in the celebratory orgy bring human beings closer to the deity

211 Caro Baroja, *Brujería vasca*, 191.
212 Reguera, 'La brujería vasca en la Edad Moderna: aquelarres, hechicería y curanderismo', pp. 240-283: p. 249.
213 Tausiet, *Ponzoña en los ojos. Brujería y superstición en Aragón en el siglo xvi*, 293.

and, according to some anthropologists, re-establishes a constant flow of energy,[214] a cathartic moment of chaos focused on restoring natural order. The *ajunt de bruxes*, in contrast, takes place not in the tangible dimension but in the spirit world. According to historian María Tausiet, the *ajunt* should be seen as a *perpetual orgy* that can always be accessed by spirits. This perpetual orgy would have no time or place, juxtaposed with the temporal orgy marked in the customary calendar.[215] Disincarnate beings would access the eternal flow of energy to maintain the balance between this world and the other, feeding off of the living and establishing harmony between light and darkness.

In its embryonic essence, the *ajunt de bruxes* echoes the idea of ecstatic journey and animal metamorphosis carried out by the spirit double, an idea originally found in shamanistic communities.[216] All of its constituent components—the activities carried out, feelings reported, teachings learned—pertain to the detachment of the bodily self, and the union of the spirit world and the realm of the supernatural. Anti-heretical discourse, ideas about the black mass, and fear of Devil worshippers clearly influenced the initial *ajunt* that dealt with ecstasy and folk beliefs about contact with the Otherworld, eventually changing Western medieval views on the spirit double and its abilities. As stated by Claude Lecouteux, even though the *ajunt* fused anti-heretical stereotypes and shamanistic traits rooted in folk culture, notions of the Double were eliminated by the church while trying to adjust to the theological view.[217] An important question emerged: how to determine which people would potentially attend the *ajunt de bruxes*. As we can deduce from accounts found in trials and folklore, birth conditions and experiential initiation could both be seen as valid means to

214 Mircea Eliade in Tausiet, *Ponzoña en los ojos. Brujería y superstición en Aragón en el siglo xvi,* 293.
215 Tausiet, *Ponzoña en los ojos. Brujería y superstición en Aragón en el siglo xvi,* 299.
216 Ginzburg, *Ecstasies,* 80.
217 Lecouteux, *Hadas, brujas y hombres lobo en la Edad Media,* 137.

acquire the ability to journey spiritually, or to be able to detach the spirit double at will. Liberation of the double necessarily required engaging in taboo activities that were expected, and later feared, by the community: cannibalism, consumption of food and drink, weather dominion.[218]

The Pyrenean *bruxa* knows no obstacles of time or space.[219] Attending the *ajunt* not only defines the *bruxa*, it also shows the irrelevance of reality, for the *bruxa* can move between this world and the other. The *ajunt* reveals the irrelevance of time; attending the perpetual orgy need not be cyclical, obeying instead the parameters of mysticism. The *ajunt* also speaks to the irrelevance of the individual before the land: only those who have cast off their own selves can access the hidden face of the Otherworld. To communicate with the dead, one must become one of them. The idea of a nocturnal gathering of supernatural beings was not forged by elites. Neither dream nor demonic hallucination, it was considered factual, a reality. The *ajunt de bruxes* represents the culmination of a greater Mystery, the ceremony in which the Glyphs of the Land, the Master Devil, and the Spirit Other conjoin. Only after completing the arduous task of progressively eliminating centuries of deeply instilled knowledge, the *bruxa* removes its many masks.

---

218 It is indeed peculiar to notice how once people started fearing and acquired a hostile behaviour against those night spirits and contact with them was forbidden in church, some of the most critical times in Europe: times of epidemics and social crisis.

219 Piniès, *Figures de la sorcellerie languedocienne*, 93.

⟋ GLOSSARY

ABBREVIATIONS

CAT   CATALAN
EUS   BASQUE
FR   FRENCH
OC   OCCITAN
SPA   SPANISH

AJUNT DE BRUIXES (CAT/OC): expression referring to the Witches' sabbat, literally 'gathering of witches'. Alternatively written as *aplec*. Corresponds to *ayuntamiento*, *junta*, or *llamamiento* (Spa), *vauderie* or *rassemblement* (Fr), and *sorginbatzarre* (Eus).

AKERBELTZ (EUS): one of the manifestations of the Devil in Basque folklore. Literally meaning the 'black billy goat' (*aker-* 'billy goat' *-beltz* 'black'), Akerbeltz is considered one of the main entities in Basque mythology, finding its origin on a possible Pyrenean goat deity called Aherbelste, formerly worshipped in the valley of Arboust (French Pyrenees).

AKELARRE/AQUELARRE (EUS): Basque word used to refer to both the witches' sabbat and the place where it took place, nowadays also used in the Spanish language. It seems akelarre was an Early Modern translation for the expression Landes du Bouc*, the 'Land of the Goat' forged by inquisitors Juan del Valle Alvarado and Pierre de Lancre in the late 16th and early 17th centuries.

ARMIER, ARMARIÉ (FR/OC): a messenger/interlocutor of the dead in the Occitane Pyrenees, verified by 14th century resources.

AZTIKERIA (EUS): divination and sorcerous arts in the Basque territories.

BEGIZKO (EUS)/ESCOMINJE (OC)/ MAL DONAT (CAT)/MALDAU (SPA)/ MAU-DAT (OC): evil eye or maleficent magic in Pyrenean regions. Known as *begizko* in Basque, *escominje* in Gascon language in the region of Béarn, *mal donat* (Cat), *maldau* in Aragon, *mau-dat* (Oc). It can be the result of envy, malefic magic, or the action of witches and other supernatural beings, and it can affect the weather, the crops, the cattle, and the health of human beings (particularly small children).

BENSOZIA (FR/OC): witch-goddess and the leader of the Wild Hunt or phantom army in Pyrenean folklore. Bensozia or Benzozia seems to be a corruption of the expression *bona socia*, 'the good partner', an euphemistic expression employed to seek the beneficial disposition of a supernatural entity, similar to Diana, Herodias, or Holda.

BITERNA (CAT): enigmatic location of the witches' sabbat in Catalan folklore, appearing for the first time in provenzal poems like *La Chanson de Roland* (11th century) and *La prise de Cordres et de Sebille* (12th century).

BOC DE BITERNA (CAT): one of the many representations of the Devil as Master of witchcraft in the Catalan Pyrenees, literally 'billy goat of Biterna'.

BRUIXONADA (CAT): Catalan term used to refer to a hailstorm caused by bruxes (the root *bruxa* is still appreciated).

BRUXA (CAT/OC/SPA): Pyrenean witch, linguistic antecessor to the Catalan *bruixa*, the Portuguese *bruxa*, the Spanish *broxa/bruja*, the Occitan *bruèisa, brèissa, broisha*, and the French *brouche* or *brouxe* (now forgotten). Originally linked with the Latin *strix*, the Germanic *hag*, and the Greek *lamia*, the bruxa is a manifestation of Otherness, a nocturnal entity which embodies opposition. Alternatively, known as *sarramauca* (Fr/Oc), *pesanta* (Cat), *pesadilla* (Spa), *inguma* (Eus) when referring to its manifestation as nightmare.

BRUXAR (CAT): an action defined by the crushing and (be)witching attributed to bruxes and their human companions.

CALABRUIX (CAT): see *bruixonada*.

CANUTET (CAT): small vessel (often a needle case) used to contain familiar spirits and often believed to be source of witch power. Known as *kuttun* or *jostorratz* (Eus).

ESCOMINJE (OC): see *begizko*.

DAME ABONDE (FR): alternative name given to Bensozia, witch-goddess and leader of the Wild Hunt in the French Pyrenees. Literally, 'Lady Abundance'.

FAYTILLERIA (OC), FETILLERIA (CAT): divination and sorcerous arts in the Pyrenean regions in particular. Those arts typically combine divinatory techniques such as hydromancy or coscinomancy (ie. divination technique employing shears and a sieve), and the usage of plants in order to discover lost things, find out about the future, or to heal/harm others. A practitioner is called *faytiller* or *fetiller*.

HECHICERÍA (SPA): see *faytilleria*.

LANDE DE BOC (FR/OC): literally, 'the land of the billy goat', first expression used to refer to the location of the *ajunt de bruxes* (13th century). Authorities like judge Pierre de Lancre would later adapt the concept and translate it freely into other languages (see *akelarre*) in order to justify widespread reach of the devil-worshipping sect of witches.

MAL DONAT (CAT), MALDAU (SPA), MAU-DAT (FR/OC): see *begizko*.

METZINA (CAT): ambivalent word referring to both medicine and poison, the role of which was considered crucial in the constitution of witchcraft as a crime during the Early Modern age. Nowadays, *metzina* is used in the Catalan language to refer exclusively to poisons and noxious substances or spells.

ORDINACIONS I PRIVILEGIS DE LES VALLS D'ÀNEU (CAT): first civil law against witchcraft in the European continent, written in the Castell de València d'Àneu (Catalan Pyrenees) in 1424. This civil law set an important precedent in Pyrenean territories, as it defined witchcraft as a crime and motivated the prosecution of certain individuals which were frowned upon by the local communities.

PONZOÑA (SPA): see *metzina*.

SORGIN (EUS): term used to designate primordial bruxes 'witches' in Basque language, alternatively written as *zorgin* or *xurguin*. In time, sorgin and its derivations would be increasingly used by the instigators and authorities in charge of the witchcraft prosecutions to designate human practitioners of folk magic and sorcery. The actual term for sorcerer and diviner in Basque language would be *azti* (see *aztikeria*).

SPIRIT DOUBLE: a manifestation of one or many parts of the human self, a literal alter ego, which detaches itself during trance, dreams, and in death. The Spirit Double can be intangible, and become one of the *bruxes* or assume the form of other people or animals.

TRIP REIAL (CAT): Catalan expression that could be translated as 'The royal tribe (or triplet)', a supernatural apparition in Catalan territories. The Trip Reial displays connections with the Three Magi and supernatural visitors who consume offerings. Nowadays, the Trip Reial still survives in the folklore of Valencia as a regional manifestation of the wild hunt.

ℊBIBLIOGRAPHY

Adell Castán, José Antonio y Celedonio García Rodríguez. "Brujas y seres mágicos de Aragón." *Dossiers feministes*, 13, 2009.

Alcoberro, Agustí. *El segle de les bruixes*. Barcelona: Barcanova, 1992.

———. 'Els Defensors de les Bruixes. La Fi de la Cacera a Catalunya', *Per Bruixa i Metzinera*. Barcelona: Museu d'Història de Catalunya, 2007.

———. 'Cacera de bruixes, justícia local i Inquisició. a Catalunya, 1487-1643: alguns criteris metodològics'. Pedralbes: *Revista d'Història Moderna*, 28. Barcelona: Universitat de Barcelona, 2008.

Amades, Joan. *Bruixes i Bruixots*. Barcelona: El Mèdol, 2002.

———. *El Mal Donat*. Barcelona: El Mèdol, 2003.

Aragonés Estella, Esperanza. *La imagen del mal en el románico Navarro*. Pamplona: Institución Príncipe de Viana, 1996.

Azurmendi, Mikel. *Nombrar, embrujar. Para una historia del sometimiento de la cultura oral en el Paiís Vasco*. Irún: Aberdania, 1993.

Barandiaran, JM. *Mitología Vasca*. San Sebastián: Txertoa, 2001.

———. *Brujería y brujas*. Donostia: Txertoa, 2012.

Baring Gould, Sabine. *The Book of Werewolves*. New York: Cosimo Books, 2008 (1865).

Bazán, Iñaki. 'Superstición y brujería en el Duranguesado a fines de la Edad Media: ¿Amboto 1507?'. *Clio & Crimen* 8. Durango: Museo de Arte e Historia de Durango, 2011.

Bordes, François. Brujos y Brujas. *Procesos de brujería en Gascuña y en el País Vasco*. Editorial Jaguar, 2006.

Braudel, Ferdinand. *The Mediterranean and the Mediterranean World in the Age of Philipp II*. translated by Sian Reynolds. Berkeley and Los Angeles, University of California Press, 1995.

Campagne, Fabián Alejandro. 'Witch or Demon? Fairies, Vampires and Nightmares in Early Modern Spain.' *Acta Ethnographica Hungarica*. An International Journal of Ethnography, 2008.

Carabia, Jacqueline. "Christianisation superficielle dans la région de Lannemezan." In: *Religion et politique dans les sociétés du Midi*. Actes du 126e Congrès national des sociétés historiques et scientifiques, 'Terres et hommes du Sud,' Toulouse, 2001. Paris: Editions du CTHS, 2002.

Cardete del Olmo, María Cruz. 'Un caso específico de teolepsia: la panolepsia.' Emerita, *Revista de Lingüística y Filología Clásica* LXXVI. Madrid: Instituto de Lenguas y Culturas del Mediterráneo y Oriente Próximo, 2008.

———. 'Entre Pan y el Diablo: el proceso de demonización del

dios Pan'. *Dialogues d'Histoire Ancienne*. Besançon: Presses Universitaires de Franche-Comté, 2015.

Cardini, Franco. *Magia, stregoneria, superstizioni nell'Occidente medievale*. Firenze: La Nuova Italia, 1972.

Caro Baroja, Julio. *Las brujas y su mundo*. Madrid: Alianza Editorial: [1966] 2006.

—*Brujería Vasca*. San Sebastián: Txertoa, 1975.

Carreras, Júlia. 2019. 'The thorn bush listens to our secrets': *Verdant Gnosis: Cultivating the Green Path* Volume 5. Revelore Press.

Castell Granados, Pau. *Orígens i evolució de la cacera de bruixes a Catalunya*. Barcelona: Universitat de Barcelona, 2013.

———. 'The Mythical Components of the Iberian Witch', *eHumanista* n.s. 26: 2014.

———. 'Wine vat witches suffocate children. The Mythical Components of the Iberian Witch'. eHumanista: Journal of Iberian Studies, vol. 25, Santa Bárbara: University of California, 2014.

———. *Bruixeria al Pallars*. Materials histórico-etnogràfics, 2018.

———. *Se'n parlave...i n'hi havie*. *Bruixeria al Pirineu i a les terres de Ponent*. Lérida: Xarxa de Museus de les Terres de Llei- da i Aran, 2019.

Chauvet, Horace. *Legendes du Roussillon*. 1899: p. 35 in Amades, Joan. Bruixes i bruixots, 2002.

Cirlot, Juan-Eduardo. *Diccionario de Símbolos*. Barcelona: Editorial Labor, 1992.

Còts e Casanha, Pèir and Caseny e Durro, Jordi. 'Actuacions en Beret ans 2009-2010 (Naut Aran, Val d'Aran)'. *Primeres Jornades D'arqueologia I Paleontologia Del Pirineu I Aran*. Lleida: Arts Gràfiques de la Diputació de Lleida, 2013.

Coutil, Léon. 'Les monuments mégalithiques des environs de Luchon'. *Bulletin de la Société Préhistorique Française* 20. Paris: Société préhistorique française, 1923.

deLabatut, Hugues. *Ordonnances et statuts synodaux du diocèse de Comenge*. Toulouse, Bovde, 1642.

De Marca, Pierre. *Histoire de Bearn, contenant l'origine des rois de Navarre, des Ducs de Gascogne, Marquis de Gothie, Princes de Bearn, Comtes de Carcassonne, de Foix, & de Bigorre, avec diverses observations geographiqves, [et] historiques, concernant principalement lesdits Païs*. Paris: Chez la Veuue Iean Camusat, 1640.

Duché-Gavet, Véronique. *Les sorcières de Pierre de Lancre*. Rev. int. estud. vascos. Cuad., 9, 2012.

Dubourg, Jacques. *Historie des sorcières et sorciers dans le Sud-Ouest*. France: Éditions Sud-Ouest, 2013.

Duvernoy, Jean. *Le Registre d'Inquisition Jacques Fournier* (Evêque de Pamiers). Paris, Mouton: 1978.

Elvira, Miguel Ángel. 'Los orígenes iconográficos del dragón medieval'. La tradición en la Antigüedad Tardía. *Antigüedad y Cristianismo*. Murcia: Universidad de Murcia, 1997.

Fernández Otal, José Antonio. 'Guirandana de Lay, hechicera, ¿bruja? y ponzoñera de Villanúa (Alto Aragon), según un proceso criminal del año 1461', *Aragon en la Edad Media*, 19. Zaragoza: Universidad de Zaragoza, 2006.

Gari Lacruz, Ángel. Brujería en Aragon'. *Actas del I Congreso de Aragón de Etnología y antropología: Tarazona, Borja, Veruela y Trasmoz 6, 7 y 8 de septiembre de 1979*. Zaragoza: Diputación de Zaragoza, Institución "Fernando el Católico", 1981.

———. 'Los aquelarres en Aragón según los documentos y la tradición oral'. *Temas de antropología aragonesa* 4. Zaragoza: Instituto Aragonés de Antropología, 1993.

———. *Brujería e Inquisición en Aragón*. Zaragoza: Delsan, 2007.

———. 'La brujería en los Pirineos (siglos XIII al XVII) Aproximación a su historia', 2010.

———. 'La posesión demoníaca en el Pirineo aragonés.' *Revista Internacional de los Estudios Vascos* 9. Donostia: Eusko Ikaskuntza, 2012.

Garmendia Larrañaga, Juan. "Sorginak, akerra eta lapurrak", Eusko Ikaskuntza, 2007.

Ghersi, Nicolas. 'Poisons, sorcières et lande de bouc', *Cahiers de recherches médiévales*, 17, 2009.

Ginzburg, Carlo. 1989. *Ecstasies. Deciphering The Witches' Sabbath.*

London: Hutchinson Radius, 1990.

Gomis, Cels. *La bruixa catalana*. Barcelona: Altafulla, 1987.

Hendrix, Scott E. "The Pursuit of Witches and the Sexual Discourse of the Sabbat." *Anthropology Magazine*, Vol. 11, Issue 2, 2011.

Henningsen, Gustav. *The Witches' Advocate: Basque Witchcraft and the Spanish Inquisition*. Reno: Nevada University Press, 1980.

———. *El abogado de las brujas. Brujería vasca e Inquisición española*. Madrid: Alianza Editorial, 1983.

———. 'El invento de la palabra "aquelarre"'. *Revista Internacional de los Estudios Vascos* 9. Donostia: Eusko Ikaskuntza, 2012.

Hernando, Josep. 'Processos inquisitorials per crim d'heretgia i una apel·lació per maltractament i parcialitat per part de l'inquisidor (1440) Documents dels protocols notarials', *Estudis Històrics i Documents dels Arxius de Protocols* 23, 2005.

Kalweit, Holger. *Dreamtime & Inner Space: The World of the Shaman*, trans. W. Wiinsche, Boston & London: Shambhala, 1988.

Kieckhefer, Richard. *La Magia en la Edad Media*. Barcelona: Editorial Crítica, 1992.

Ladurie, Emmanuel Le Roy. *Montaillou: The Promised Land of Error* (30th Anniversary ed.). New York, George Braziller, 2008.

Lamarca, Genaro. *El Valle de Aísa*. Zaragoza: Mira Editores, 1993.

Lavenia Vincenzo, "The Alpine Model of Witchcraft: the Italian Context in the Early Modern Period." In *Communities and Conflicts in the Alps: from the Late Middle Ages to Early Modernity* (ed. Marco Bellabarba, Hannes Obermair, Hitomi Sato. Bologna: Il Mulino).

Lecouteux, Claude. *Hadas, Brujas, y Hombres Lobo en la Edad Media: Historia del Doble*. Palma de Mallorca: José J. de Olañeta, 2005.

———. *Return of the Dead: Ghosts, Ancestors, and the Transparent Veil in the Pagan Mind*. Rochester, Inner Traditions, 2009.

———. *Phantom Armies of the Night*. Rochester: Inner Traditions, 2011.

Libros del Cuentamiedos, Brujas en el Pirineo Fantástico, 2006.

Lisón Tolosana, Carmelo. *Las brujas en la historia de España*. Madrid: Temas de Hoy, 1992.

Lladonosa Pujol, José. *El cas singular de na Valentina Guarner del Anecdotari de l'Estudi General de Lleida*. Lleida, Virgili de Pagés, 1988.

Macias Cárdenas, Francisco Javier. 'El mito del hombre lobo en la Edad Media'. *Ubi Sunt?* 28. Cádiz: Universidad de Cádiz, 2013.

Magliocco, Sabina. "Witchcraft, Healing and Vernacular Magic in Italy." In *Witchcraft Continued: Popular magic in modern Europe*. Manchester University Press, 2004.

Mallory, J. P.; Adams, Douglas, et al. *Encyclopedia of Indo-European Culture*. London: Fitzroy Dearborn Publishers, 1997.

Martínez de Lezea, Toti. *Leyendas de Euskal Herria*. Donostia: Erein Argitaletxea, 2004.

Martínez Pisón, Maria. 'Herensuge, Edensuge, Iransuge'. *Por encima de todas las Zarzas,* 2017.

Marliave, Olivier. *Pequeño Diccionario de Mitología Vasca y Pirenaica*. Palma de Mallorca: José J. De Olañeta, 1995.

———. *Trésor de la Mythologie Pyréenne*. Bordeaux: Éditions Sud Ouest, 2005.

———. *Dictionnaire de magie et de sorcellerie dans les Pyrénées*. Luçon: Éditions Sud-Ouest, 2006.

Martin, Élisabeth and Fuchs, Magali. *Monographie Historique Site Du Bloc Erratique Dit Caillaou D'arriba Pardin*. Midi-Pyrénées: DREAL, 2011.

Martínez de Lezea, Toti. *Leyendas de Euskal Herria*. Donostia: Erein Argitaletxea, 2004.

Martínez Pisón, Maria. 'Herensuge, Edensuge, Iransuge'. *Por encima de todas las Zarzas,* 2017.

Martínez Pisón, María. [Online] 'Etorkizuna, kontakizuna,' 2016. Available at: https://porencimadetodaslaszarzas.wordpress.com/2016/09/29/etorkizuna-kontakizuna/ (Accessed: 10 December 2019)

Muraro, Luisa. "Ir libremente entre sueño y realidad". *Acta historica et archaeologica mediaevalia*, no. 19, 1998.

Nieto, Manuel Fernandez. *Proceso a la brujería. En torno al auto de fe de los brujos de ugarramurdi, Logroño, 1610.* Madrid: Tecnos 1989.

Padilla Lapuente, José Ignacio. *L'esperit d'Àneu. Liibre dels costums i ordinacions de les Valls d'Àneu.* Esterri d'Àneu. Consell Cultural de les Valls d'Àneu, 1999.

Parker, Robert. *On Greek Religion.* New York: Cornell University Press, 2011.

Pastor i Castillo, Robert. *Aquí les penjaven.* Andorra: Consell General d'Andorra, 2004.

Piniès, Jean-Pierre. *Figures de la sorcellerie languedocienne.* París: Éditions du CNRS, 1983.

———. 'Pet-sus-fuèlha ou le départ des sorcières pour le sabbat'. *Heresis* nos. 44–45. Carcassonne: Centre d'Etudes Cathares, 2006.

Rampton, Martha. *European Magic and Witchcraft: A Reader* (Readings in Medieval Civilizations and Cultures). University of Toronto Press, 2018.

Reguera, Iñaki. 'La brujería vasca en la Edad Moderna: aquelarres, hechicería y curanderismo'. *Revista Internacional de los Estudios Vascos.* Issue 9. Donostia: Eusko Ikaskuntza, 2012.

Rilova Jericó, Carlos. 'Las últimas brujas de Europa—Acusaciones de brujería en el País Vasco', Vasconia: *Cuadernos de historia—geografía* 32. Donostia: Eusko-Ikaskuntza, 2002.

———. "Indicios para una Historia Nocturna vasca. Brujas, brujos y paganos en el País Vasco." *Zainak.* 28, 2006.

Risco, Vicente. *Satanás, historia del Diablo.* Barcelona: Aymá: pp. 189–190 in Gari Lacruz, Ángel. 2007. Brujería e Inquisición en Aragón. Zaragoza: Editorial Delsan, 1956.

Roques, Patrice. *Sorcellerie et superstitions dans les Pyrénées centrales du XVIe au XIXe siècle.* Nimes: Lacour Éditeur, 2002.

Russell, Jeffrey Burton. *Witchcraft in the Middle Ages.* Ithaca, NY: Cornell University Press, 1984.

———. *The Devil, Perceptions of Evil from Antiquity to Primitive Christianity.* New York: Cornell University Press, 1990.

Sacaze, Julien. *Epigraphie de Luchnon.* Paris: Didier et cie. Editeurs, 1880.

Segura Urra, Félix. "Hechicería y brujería en la Navarra medieval". *Rev. int. estud. vascos. Cuaderno* 9, 2012.

Soler i Amigó, Joan. *Enciclopèdia de la Fantasia Popular Catalana.* Barcelona: Barcanova, 1998.

Tausiet, María. *Brujería y superstición en Aragón en el siglo XVI.* Zaragoza: Universidad de Zaragoza, 1997.

———. *Ponzoña en los ojos.* Madrid: Turner, 2004.

Tchérémissinoff, Yaramila; Bruxelles, Laurent; Lagarrigue, Anne et al. 'Le tumulus de l'Estaque 2, commune d'Avezac-Prat-Lahitte (Hautes-Pyrénées): résultats de fouille préventive'. *Archéologie des Pyrénées Occidentales et des Landes,* Groupe Archéologique des Pyrénées Occidentales, 2008.

Tilander, Gunnar and Vidal Mayor. *Traducción aragonesa de la obra In Excelsis Dei Thesauris de Vidal de Canellas*. Lund, Hakan Ohlssons, 1956.

Tilbury, Gervasius Von. *Otia imperialia. De phantasiis, nocturnis opiniones XCIII*. Hannover: Rümpler, 1856.

Tolosana, Carmelo Lisón. *Las brujas en la historia de España*. Madrid: Temas de Hoy, 1992.

Trevor-Roper, Hugh. *The European Witch Craze of the Sixteenth and Seventeenth Centuries: and Other Essays*. New York: Harper and Row, 1967.

Usunáriz Garayoa, Jesús María. 'La caza de brujas en la Navarra moderna (siglos XVI–XVII)'. *Revista Internacional de los Estudios Vascos*. Issue 9. Donostia: Eusko Ikaskuntza, 2012.

Valls i Oliva, Àlvar and Carol i Romàn, Roser. *Llegendes d'Andorra*. Barcelona: Abadia de Montserrat, 2010.

Ventura, Jordi. 1960. 'El catarismo en Cataluña'. *Boletín de la Real Academia de Buenas Letras de Barcelona*, 28 (1959–60): pp. 100–101 in Castell, Pau. 2013.

Orígens i evolució de la cacera de bruixes a Catalunya. Barcelona: Universitat de Barcelona.

Vinyoles Vidal, Teresa. 'Metgesses, llevadores, fetilleres, fascinadores...: bruixes a l'edat mitjana'. *Per Bruixa i Metzineria. La cacera de bruixes a Catalunya*. Barcelona: Museu d'Història de Catalunya, 2007.

———. 'Llevadores, guaridores i fetilleres. Exemples de sabers i pràctiques femenines a la Catalunya medieval', *Études Roussillonnaises, Revue d'Histoire et d'archéologie Méditerranéennes* 26, 2013–2014.

Violant i Simorra, Ramon. *Etnologia Pallaresa*. Tremp: Escudella, 1981.

Wilby, Emma. *Cunning Folk and Familiar Spirits: Shamanistic Visionary Traditions in Early Modern British Witchcraft and Magic*. Eastbourne: Sussex Academic Press, 2005.

———. 'Burchard's strigae, the Witches' Sabbath, and Shamanistic Cannibalism in Early Modern Europe' *Magic, Ritual, and Witchcraft*. Philadelphia: University of Pennsylvania Press, 2013.

❡INDEX

This first edition of *LAND OF THE GOAT* was published by Three Hands Press on 15 August, 2024. It consists of 2,000 softcover copies, 1,000 standard hardcover copies in colour dust wraps, a deluxe edition of 29 hand-numbered editions in black goatskin with marbled endpapers and slipcase, and a special edition of 13 copies in full red goatskin with marbled endpapers and slipcase. Fine bindings were executed by Andy Rottner.

✝

Scribae Quo Mysterivm Famvlatvr